PREPARING ADMINISTRATIVE MANUALS

PREPARING ADMINISTRATIVE MANUALS

Susan Z. Diamond

A DIVISION OF AMERICAN MANAGEMENT ASSOCIATIONS

Library of Congress Cataloging in Publication Data

Diamond, Susan Z
   Preparing administrative manuals.

   Includes index.
   1. Management--Handbooks, manuals, etc. I. Title.
HD31.D498   650'.028   80-69692
ISBN 0-8144-5631-6   AACR1

© 1981 AMACOM
A division of American Management Associations, New York.

FOURTH PRINTING

To Allan

Foreword

THIS BOOK will give you a complete system for preparing any type of administrative manual. The principles outlined here work for both large and small companies, and for both profit and not-for-profit organizations. In this book are the tools and knowledge you need to prepare an administrative manual. Your job is to adapt this information to fit your particular situation and to produce a manual that will increase your organization's effectiveness.

The guidelines in this book were developed through years of teaching seminars for the American Management Associations, through reviewing hundreds of different corporate manuals, through talking with the preparers of these manuals, and, of course, through personal experience in developing manuals. I owe a great deal to the participants in those seminars and to the organizations I have consulted with. Not only was the exchange of ideas always rewarding, but the continued interest in and requests for this book were tremendous motivators for me.

Susan Z. Diamond

Contents

CHAPTER 1

Why Prepare a Manual?

DURING THE PAST DECADE, the number of corporate administrative manuals has multiplied rapidly. Most organizations larger than the mom-and-pop hotdog stand have policy manuals, departmental procedures manuals, personnel manuals, and systems manuals. Some even have manuals on how to write manuals. One firm I worked with wasn't even sure how many manuals it had; an inventory revealed over 200 different ones.

The inevitable question arises: Are these manuals simply another example of the multiplication of paperwork in most organizations, or do they serve a useful purpose? The answer depends on the manual.

Properly designed and used, manuals can be valuable corporate communications tools. Poorly developed and written manuals are simply a waste of money. Unfortunately, most manuals belong in the second category. Too few organizations have planned their manuals as a coherent system that recognizes the various user groups' interests.

Manuals are a highly specialized communications medium and they require specialized communications skills—skills that are not normally taught in school or on the job. This book has been written to teach those skills. It will show you in simple, logical steps how to develop usable manuals—not dust catchers—that will save your organization time and money.

Let's begin by answering a question frequently asked by top management: "Why does my company need manuals?" Here are eight good reasons why:

1. Manuals give every user a standard, common reference sys-

tem. Everyone has exactly the same information and is operating under the same rules.

2. Manuals provide documentation. A manual spells out the organization's policies and procedures so that this information is no longer simply stored in a few people's heads. This vital information is not lost when these key people leave the company. Moreover, by developing a manual, a company is often forced to clarify vague or poorly defined policies and to simplify complex procedures.

3. A manual serves as a portable, easy-to-use filing system. Answers to questions can be found quickly and easily without rummaging through countless file folders.

4. Manuals have clout. A corporate policy clearly stated in an official manual has more impact than a three-year-old memo buried somewhere in a file or a memo whose originator has left the company.

5. Manuals help users comply with the policies of the federal government and other regulatory groups. EEO, ERISA, OSHA, and the Foreign Corrupt Practices Act are just a few of the laws that require documentation of specific policies and procedures. In fact, these laws have been the impetus for many manuals. Hospitals document their procedures in manuals to meet the requirements of the Joint Commission on the Accreditation of Hospitals. The Federal Aviation Agency and the Civil Aeronautics Board place similar requirements on airlines.

6. Manuals save time and ensure accurate responses. Employees can "check the book" rather than ask someone who may or may not know the correct answer.

7. Manuals serve as training tools for new employees, helping them to learn the job correctly at the start. Many manuals are developed specifically as training aids.

8. Manuals reduce paperwork by consolidating information in one place.

TYPES OF MANUALS

There are nearly as many different kinds of manuals as there are reasons for writing them. Some of the principal types of manuals are:

Policy. The cornerstone of most manual systems, the policy manual spells out the rules of the organization. Policy manuals state the company's ten (or ten thousand) commandments, such as "Whenever possible, available positions will be filled from within the company" or "Employees of Wizard Widgets shall not accept bribes."

Procedures. A procedures manual is a how-to book. "Adding a new account to the general ledger" and "settling a customer's damage claim" are examples of procedures. Procedures manuals are sometimes known as operations manuals.

Policy and procedures. A combination of the two preceding categories, this type of manual has its own special problems. In large organizations, it often becomes extremely bulky and unwieldy. For this reason, separate policy and procedures manuals are frequently preferable. In very small organizations or in a single department, however, the two can sometimes be combined in one binder.

When policies and procedures are combined, they should be in separate sections with the policies taking precedence. Intermingling the two confuses the user and diminishes the importance of the policies. Also, policies and procedures don't always "match up." For example, there is no procedure for the policy of not accepting bribes. And there is generally no policy for a procedure on operating a particular machine.

Policy and procedures manuals sometimes can be "modularized"—that is, employees are given only those sections (or modules) of the manual that pertain to their position. For example, one set of employees might receive a policy section and an accounting procedures section, while another set receives the policy section plus a purchasing procedures section. A third set of employees might receive all three sections. This system cuts costs and makes the manual smaller and less formidable for employees.

If you decide to modularize, keep the system simple. Don't give employees only those procedures in a section that apply to them; you'll end up having to evaluate each procedure's relevance to each employee. Instead, limit yourself to a modular breakdown: either employees get everything in a module or they get nothing.

Training or instructional. These how-to manuals are generally more detailed than procedures manuals. The assumption behind a training manual is that the user has little, if any, prior knowledge of the subjects covered. For example, a training manual might instruct the employee to turn on the computer terminal and "sign on," while a procedures manual would omit that instruction and begin with the first active step in the process. Training manuals may also use programmed learning techniques or self-check quizzes to test the user's understanding of the material.

Reference. Some manuals are used primarily as reference tools. Such manuals might contain supply or equipment lists, account service requirements, or any information (other than policies or procedures) that employees must refer to occasionally.

PREPARING A MANUAL

The first step in preparing a manual is determining what you want to accomplish. To do this, ask yourself the following questions:

What is the organization's objective in creating this manual? The organization may be introducing a new computerized accounting system. Or it may wish to ensure that all managers follow certain personnel policies and procedures.

What benefits will the manual provide to its users? The manual may enable users to learn the new accounting system quickly and easily, or it may be a ready reference source for personnel questions.

What do I (or my department) hope to accomplish with this manual? In addition to meeting the organization's objectives, the manual should also help your department. With a manual in existence, you may have to answer fewer questions and do less troubleshooting.

Once you have determined the manual's objectives, put them in writing. This will help you clarify your thoughts and make sure they are logical. Remember that each manual has its unique reasons for being. And only if you develop good answers for these questions should you create the manual.

As you determine your manual's objectives, remember that all manuals have one common goal: to get results. The purpose of the manual is to ensure that its users behave in a particular way, whether that involves obeying company rules or following a specific procedure. If your manual achieves this goal, it is a definite success.

CHAPTER 2

Planning: The Key to Success

CAREFUL PLANNING is essential if you are to produce a manual that meets its users' needs, that is worth the time and money spent, and that is distributed on schedule. In this chapter, you'll learn some general planning pointers that will simplify your efforts. Then we'll examine two key aspects of the planning process: preparation for the writing and the mechanics of production. Finally, we'll take a look at the nemesis of many manual planners: the budget.

WHOSE RESPONSIBILITY?

Let's begin by examining where in the organization the responsibility for producing manuals lies. In other words, who's going to do the planning—and all the work that follows?

Developers of manuals do not fit neatly on the organization chart the way treasurers and personnel managers do. At times they are found in the administrative services area or in corporate communications. But all too frequently they are scattered throughout the organization, with each department producing its own manuals.

When manual development is not centralized, the organization often ends up with a proliferation of manuals of all sizes and shapes. Generally, each manual has its own format, layout, and style. What's worse, the manuals sometimes contradict each other. To add one more item to this catalog of disasters, key areas such as finance often don't even have manuals—here, people are too busy to produce them.

The solution to these problems is the creation of a centralized department for the production of manuals. Not only does such a department bring order out of chaos but, more important, it provides professional writing skills and expertise in manuals production. Also, the department eliminates contradictions and duplicate efforts.

When I propose this solution, one objection is usually raised: "A centralized department doesn't *know* enough to write manuals for accounting, personnel, and all the other departments." Here's my answer: Professional writers collect the appropriate material from each department (see Chapter 3). Their job is to structure and edit the material, not to tell accounting how to do its job. As a further safeguard, qualified people from each department review the manuals so no inaccuracies slip through. Thus the manuals become a team effort.

As to which department should be responsible for the production of manuals, generally either administrative services or corporate communications is a logical choice. I have a slight preference for people in corporate communications, because they are more likely to have the needed writing skills.

If centralizing responsibility for the manuals is simply not feasible, the organization should at least coordinate the efforts of the various groups producing manuals. Establish a manuals committee to meet once a month to discuss each group's activities and share ideas. The committee should develop general guidelines for style and format and possibly even prepare a company guidebook on production. When a coordinating committee reviews the various manuals, duplication of effort and contradictory information are avoided.

PLANNING POINTERS

Here are a few pointers on planning your manual.

1. *Allow plenty of time for planning.* You'll save time in the long run. Unless you plan carefully and thoroughly, you're likely to encounter many time-consuming problems. For example, you might find that you can't meet your deadline because the vice president who is to review your manual is inspecting the company's European plants for two weeks. Or you might learn, too late, that the word processing center is converting to new equipment and will be operating at reduced efficiency for the next six weeks. Planning won't prevent the vice president from going or the center from

changing equipment. However, if you're aware of these situations ahead of time, you can adjust your plans to compensate.

2. *Have others review your plans.* The review should include not only your supervisor, whose approval may be mandatory, but also people who've actually produced manuals or who will be heavily involved in your manual.

3. *Confirm all estimates of time, money, and personnel in writing.* Many people give verbal estimates "off the top of their heads" and subsequently forget they gave them. Getting a written estimate or confirming a verbal estimate in writing shows that you're taking the estimate seriously and will be planning on it. Also, if there's a disagreement later, a written statement may be helpful.

4. *Plan now for updates.* Even the best manual will need revisions and updates within six months after its distribution. Planning now will help ensure that when revisions are due, the necessary time and money are available.

5. *Anticipate problems.* You'll find that troubleshooting problems ahead of time pays big dividends. Make a list of the problems you anticipate, based on your knowledge of the organization. For example, a key problem may be a print shop that never meets a deadline, an employee who is unlikely to cooperate in supplying data, or your own lack of time to work on the project. Analyze each problem and find a way to prevent or resolve it. The following chapters will examine many of the most common problems and suggest ways to deal with them.

PLANNING THE WRITING

The first step in planning the writing is defining the subject matter: What is the manual going to be about? It's easier to define the subject if you list all the manual's potential user groups and then determine what information they need. Also keep in mind the manual's objectives, which you determined in Chapter 1.

After you've tentatively defined the subject area, get some feedback from the manual's users. Is the subject too broad? Too narrow? Remember that a manual cannot be all things to all people. A personnel manual may cover those policies and procedures used by members of the personnel department, or it may cover those personnel policies and procedures that all managers in the organization must know. Once you're satisfied with your definition of the scope of the manual, have it approved by the people who will eventually have to approve the final manual. This will help prevent major problems when you're further along in the manual's development.

The second step in planning the writing is determining who will collect the data. You have two main alternatives:

1. You or your staff collect the data.
2. The user departments collect the data and submit it to the writers.

The pros and cons of each approach are examined in detail in Chapter 3.

The third step in planning the writing is deciding who will write the manual. Again you have two main alternatives:

1. The user departments write the manual and you or your staff edit it.
2. You or your staff write the manual.

A lack of resources in your department may force you to choose the first alternative. However, the second one is definitely preferable. When nonprofessional writers prepare the material, extensive editing is usually required. The editing can be almost as time consuming as writing the material yourself. And the end product is seldom as high in quality as a manual written by experienced writers.

Whichever alternative you select, the ultimate editorial responsibility should rest with one person, not a group. This approach has three advantages:

1. The manual has a unified, consistent style and tone. This uniformity increases the manual's readability, as users become accustomed to one style.
2. One person has the decision-making authority. You've probably heard the old quip: "A camel is a horse built by a committee." Writing by committee is as uneven as the camel's hump.
3. Reviewers have to deal with only one person. It's easier for a reviewer to discuss changes or comments with one person than with a team of writers.

The final step in planning the writing is establishing a timetable. If possible, allow ample time for the writing process. When writers hurry, the quality of their work declines.

I've learned through years of writing and constant struggles to meet deadlines that I always underestimate the time it takes to complete a writing project. Most of the writers I know share this failing. So if you're doing the writing yourself, multiply your original estimate by one and a half. If someone else is doing the writing, apply the same rule to their estimate unless you *know* that they consistently meet their deadlines.

As you see, I'm advocating that the writer set the deadline. I firmly believe that people are more receptive to deadlines set by themselves and more responsible in meeting them.

PLANNING THE MECHANICS OF PRODUCTION

After you have made preparations for the writing, begin planning the other aspects of production. The first item on your list should be developing an efficient clearance and review process. You need to determine who must approve the manual before production and how long it will take to get these approvals. (The various aspects of the review process are discussed in detail in Chapter 9.)

Your next task is to decide on the manual's layout, format, and binders. In other words, you're determining the manual's physical appearance. (Chapters 4 and 5 explain the various decisions you'll have to make.) A word of warning: Binders often must be ordered six or more weeks in advance, so don't delay your decision on this question.

You should also determine how the manual will be printed and how many copies you'll want to order. (Chapter 9 gives guidelines on this subject.)

Another key step in the production planning process is establishing a central control point. One person should coordinate the entire process, making sure that everyone and everything is either on schedule or as close to schedule as is possible. The position of coordinator requires an eye for detail, organizational skill, and an ability to work well with different types of people. Ideally, the coordinator should have been with the organization for a few years and should know reasonably well most of the people he or she will be working with.

Who should be the central control point? There's no one right answer. In smaller organizations, the person who writes the manual may also serve as the control point. In larger organizations, the manuals department may have a "manuals coordinator" or "manuals administrator" whose primary job is to serve as a central control point for all manuals and their updates.

The last step in planning the mechanical aspects of production is developing a work schedule. At this point, you should have time estimates for writing, reviewing, printing, and all other aspects of production. Your job now is to assemble those bits and pieces of information into a complete schedule.

Two scheduling techniques are particularly successful for manuals—PERT and milestone charts. These techniques work well separately, but they are most effective when used together.

PERT stands for Program Evaluation and Review Technique. The U.S. Navy Special Projects Office and Booz Allen & Hamilton, a management consulting firm, originally developed PERT for the Polaris missile program. At about the same time, the Du Pont Corporation developed another planning technique called CPM (Critical Path Method). The two techniques were eventually merged into the system we now call PERT. With this history, PERT may sound rather formidable; however, it is really just a project flowchart with time values attached.

Preparing a PERT chart for a manual is relatively simple, and the chart is an invaluable aid in organizing the work flow. Here's how to develop a PERT chart and to determine the critical path—the minimum time required to complete the project.

1. Divide the preparation of the manual into a number of small steps. Each step will occupy a separate square on the PERT chart.

2. Determine the sequence in which the activities must be performed. Remember that many activities, such as collecting data from several different sources, can be performed during the same time period.

3. Diagram the sequence in flowchart form. Figure 1, a sample PERT chart for a manual, illustrates the flowcharting technique.

4. Determine a time estimate in workdays or workweeks for each

Figure 1. Sample PERT chart.

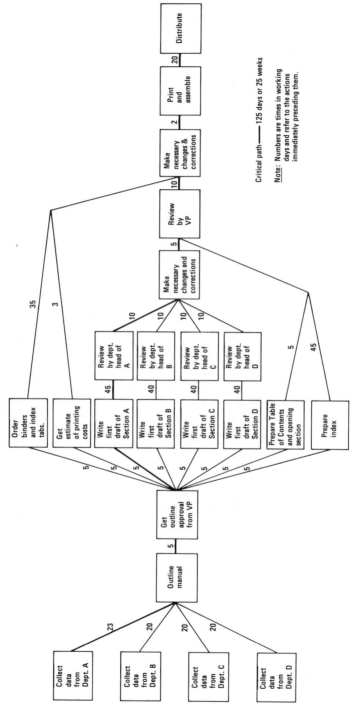

step on the chart. Figure 1 is done in workdays, but you may find weeks easier to work with.

5. Write a time estimate for each step on the chart. In Figure 1, the time estimates are on the connecting lines following each step.

6. Determine the total time needed to complete each path on the chart.

The path with the greatest total time requirement is the critical path (the boldface line in Figure 1). This is the minimum amount of time in which the manual can be completed. Any delay in carrying out an activity on the critical path will delay the manual's completion. All other paths have slack time—the time difference between the critical path and a noncritical path. Slack time can be very helpful. If you get behind schedule in a noncritical path, you know exactly how much leeway you have before the manual goes off schedule.

Another valuable scheduling technique in planning manuals is the milestone chart. To prepare a milestone chart (see Figure 2), you again divide the manual's development into a number of small steps. Use a line with an open triangle (──△) to indicate the estimated time in weeks needed to complete each step. Thicken the line (━━△) to indicate the actual, not the projected, progress. When the activity is completed, shade in the triangle (━━▲). To indicate rescheduling, extend the line and add a square at the end (──△──□). When the activity is completed, shade in the square (━━△━■). If activities are rescheduled, attach a brief explanation to the chart.

You can use a milestone chart in the same way as a PERT chart for planning the entire development process. However, unlike a PERT chart, the milestone chart does not show the interrelationships of the various steps in the process. For this reason, the PERT chart is generally preferable as an overall planning tool.

The milestone chart is most effective for planning each person's role in creating the manual. Everyone involved in the project should have a milestone chart for his or her responsibilities so that each person's progress (or lack thereof) is clearly identifiable. Consequently, in at least one company, the charts are known as "millstones."

When milestone charts are used to measure individual perfor-

Figure 2. Milestone chart.

| FUNCTION _____ | | INDIVIDUAL _____ |

ACTIVITY	WEEK ENDING	JAN 4 11 18 25	FEB 1 8 15 22 29	MAR 7 14 21 28	APR 4 11 18 25	MAY 2 9 16 23 30	JUNE 6 13 20 27	JULY 4 11 18 25	AUG 1 8 15 22 29	SEPT 5 12 19 26	OCT 3 10 17 24 31	NOV 7 14 21 28	DEC 5 12 19 26

Scheduled activity time span _____

Actual activity progress _____

Rescheduled activity _____

Completed activity _____ ◄

Completed rescheduled activity _____ ◄

mance and a PERT chart to measure overall progress, the result is a complete system for planning and control.

Milestone and PERT charts are also effective tools for reporting to management on the manual's progress. In fact, the very existence of a PERT chart shows management that you've planned carefully and know what you're doing. You may even want to post a large PERT chart on the wall of your office and shade in the completed paths. Then everyone can see the current state of affairs and the importance of his or her efforts in creating the manual.

BUDGETING

Budgeting is the final step in planning your manual. Unfortunately, there are no easy guidelines for budgeting a manual—no simple formula of x dollars per page. However, if you've planned carefully, budgeting should be fairly straightforward. When you obtain the time estimates for each step in the process, also request a cost estimate (where appropriate) and a statement of how long the estimate will be effective. Some of the areas where you will need a cost estimate are binders, tabs, printing, graphics, and typesetting. This information will form the basis for your budget.

The costs included in your budget will depend on your organization's budgeting system. Some organizations charge all interdepartmental costs back to the department requesting the work. For example, if the graphic arts department designs cover art for the manual, you will be charged for that department's labor and expenses. Other organizations will charge your department only for the outside or additional expenses required to produce the manual.

Whatever your organization's system, your biggest problem, especially if you are new to manuals production, will be remembering to include all relevant costs. To help you, here are two lists, one of possible general cost items and one of potential people costs (the time of those people who will be helping you).

General Costs
    Binders
    Communications (correspondence, telephone)
    Distribution costs (If the manuals are to be mailed or shipped, be

sure to include the cost of labeling and packaging, as well as postage and shipping charges.)
Graphics (cover art, diagrams, sketches, special charts)
Index tabs
Paper
Printing
Travel (may be required to collect data)
Typing or typesetting

Personnel Time Costs
Data collector(s)
Data suppliers
Coordinator of manual
Reviewers
Typists or word processing personnel
Writer(s)

Here are some pointers on preparing your budget. First get all estimates in writing. Then double-check the estimates and question any that appear suspiciously low. In one company, a communications failure between the purchasing department and the print shop resulted in a price quote for 1,000 tabs instead of 1,000 sets of six tabs. That incident demolished the budget for the manual!

Remember that most estimates for outside services such as binders and printing are good for only a specific time period. So reconfirm the estimate if it appears that you won't be using the service within the quoted period.

Be sure that you budget now for updates. You will need to make them and they are often costly. Moreover, if you don't budget for updates now, you may not be able to afford them later. Finally, when you present the budget to management, include your PERT chart in the presentation. Then management can see easily how each cost relates to the production process and why each cost is necessary.

CHAPTER 3

Collecting and Organizing the Data

AFTER YOU'VE COMPLETED the planning process, you're ready to begin gathering and organizing all the information that is to be included in the manual.

METHODS OF DATA COLLECTION

Normally you'll collect the information you need through one or more of these methods: research, observation, written questionnaires, and interviews. Let's consider the pros and cons of each method, as well as the situations where you'd be most likely to use each.

Research

With manuals, the term "research" does not mean long hours in the stacks of the public library. Instead, it means long hours in the files of your organization. If your organization has not developed manuals before and has communicated its policies and procedures through bulletins, memos, newsletters, and other means, your first task will be to locate all documents containing information that should be in the manual.

If your organization lacks manuals, it also probably lacks a comprehensive records management program. If so, you or your staff must ferret out all relevant documents. This task will be greatly simplified if you can locate one or two "packrats"—long-service employees who have saved every document that has ever entered their in-boxes. A search of their files should reveal most, if not all, of the documents you need.

Another fertile area for research is the mailroom or print shop. One of these departments will usually have copies of all documents that have been printed and distributed internally. However, don't depend exclusively on this source; only documents reproduced in the print shop will be on file.

After you've collected what will probably be a mountain of paper, sort it according to subject. Then put the documents under each subject in chronological order, with the latest papers on top. Weed out all documents that have been superseded. Now you have a hard core of data to work with.

Observation

Observation is exactly what the name implies: observing someone perform a particular procedure and writing down all of his or her actions in the correct sequence. This approach is especially helpful when the people who normally perform the procedure have difficulty explaining what they do.

Begin by developing a rapport with the people you are observing. Make it clear that you are observing them because they are experts at their jobs, not because you want to "catch" them in an error. Spend enough time with them so they feel at ease in your presence. Then begin taking notes and asking questions about any steps you don't understand.

Observation is an enjoyable way to collect data—you get to know people in the organization you would not have met otherwise, and in some situations, it is the only effective method. However, it is also one of the most time-consuming data collection methods.

Written Questionnaires

Written questionnaires are useful when you need to collect specific information from a large number of people. For example, you might use a questionnaire to find out how each department handles basic personnel situations for which no official policy exists. The questionnaire answers can help the organization determine a policy. Questionnaires also can be used to determine what information users would like to see in a manual.

Despite the value of questionnaires, they do have several draw-backs. They are impersonal, and they do not encourage respondents to provide additional information. Also, many people return questionnaires only after some prodding. Even so, in very large organizations where other forms of data collection are not practical, questionnaires are often essential.

If you do use a questionnaire for data collection, keep it as short and simple as possible. The easier the questionnaire is to complete, the more likely your respondents are to complete it.

Interviewing

Conducting an interview seems to give people more difficulty than any other form of data collection. This is unfortunate, because interviewing is one of the most comprehensive and enjoyable ways to collect data if you follow these guidelines:

1. *Be sure you're interviewing the right person.* The right person means the individual with the information you need. This person is not necessarily a department head; he or she may be anyone with a day-to-day working knowledge of the subject.

In your eagerness to reach the right person, don't neglect the corporate courtesies. Don't interview someone in another department without clearing the interview with the appropriate manager. You may even need to interview a department head or manager briefly to assuage his or her ego before you can talk to the person with the knowledge you need.

2. *Schedule the interview well in advance, and explain its purpose to the interviewee.* This gives the interviewee time to gather any information or documents you may need and time to organize his or her ideas on the subject. Also, it's common courtesy.

3. *Allow ample time for the interview.* Obviously the length of the interview will depend on the amount of material you have to obtain. But it's better to schedule more time than you need and end the interview early than to have to rush. If you hurry, you may miss some key information and end up having to schedule a second interview.

4. *Make sure you will not be interrupted during the interview.* If possible, conduct the interview in a conference room or other "neutral" area so that you will not be interrupted by phone calls or by staff members dropping in with a "quick" question. If this setting is not

possible, try to hold the interview in your office. Then arrange for your secretary to hold calls and prevent other interruptions.

5. *Prepare a list of written questions before the interview.* If you try to conduct the interview without adequate preparation, you'll probably miss some key points and you may appear disorganized to the interviewee. Do not submit the questions to the interviewee in advance. This destroys spontaneity and tends to limit discussion.

6. *Take the list of questions to the interview to make sure you gather all the information you need.* This way you won't call the interviewee later and say, "I'm sorry but I forgot to ask you a few things." Also, taking the list eliminates awkward lulls in the conversation: either you have another question to ask or it's time to end the interview.

Try to ask the questions in logical order, but don't be disturbed if the interviewee answers the questions in a different order. Let the interviewee follow the natural flow of his or her thoughts. When there's a pause in the conversation, return to one of the skipped questions. Just be sure you cover all the questions before the interview ends.

7. *Remember that you, not the interviewee, are conducting the interview.* Some interviewees may try to take control or may launch into a monologue that's unconnected with the subject. Don't be afraid to break in, politely but firmly, with a remark like "That's very interesting; I'd no idea that happened. Now I do need to know how you feel about the topic we were discussing." At the same time, don't confine the interviewee too rigidly to your questions. You may gain some valuable information from his or her side remarks. And some small talk may make the interview flow more smoothly.

8. *Take thorough notes or tape-record the interview.* Taping is generally more accurate than note taking and allows you to concentrate on interviewing instead of on writing things down. However, if you're going to tape an interview, be sure to get the interviewee's permission ahead of time. And remember that the interviewee has the right to refuse permission.

You may find that some interviewees who give permission for taping are nevertheless inhibited by the recorder. A few people who speak fluently in direct conversation can hardly say a word when a tape recorder is on. So if people are clearly uncomfortable with the recorder, turn it off and take notes instead.

If you do take notes, review them as soon as possible after the interview is over. Be sure they are readable and include all pertinent information. It's much easier to add details while the interview is fresh in your mind.

9. *Use "active listening" to ensure understanding.* Active listening is rephrasing the interviewee's remarks in your own words to verify your understanding. Use an opening like "Does this mean that . . . ?" or "Do I have this right?" and then restate the information in your own words. Obviously, you needn't rephrase every remark your interviewees make (they'd begin to question your sanity). But do paraphrase whenever you're not sure if you understand someone and whenever you want to doublecheck what the interviewee said. Here are a few additional tips on good listening:

Maintain eye contact with the speaker.
Use low-level responses such as "uh-huh," "yes," or a nod of the head to indicate your understanding.
Give the speaker 100 percent of your attention.

10. *As soon as possible after the interview, send a memo summarizing the main points of your discussion to the interviewee for confirmation.* It's much easier to correct an error at this stage than after the first draft of the manual is written. And you're less likely to omit important details if you write up the interview promptly. In the memo, also thank the interviewee for his or her cooperation.

WHO SHOULD COLLECT THE DATA?

So far we've been discussing the "how-to's" of data collection—research, observation, questionnaires, and interviews. Now let's take a look at the "who's."

Either the writer of the manual or people from the user departments can collect the data. Each approach has its advantages and disadvantages. When the writer collects the data, he or she acquires a thorough understanding of the subject before beginning to write. This approach generally produces a superior manual—one that is both accurate and well written. Also, because the writer is *not* an expert, he or she is likely to include information that experts on the subject would omit because they assume it is "common knowledge."

The primary drawback to this approach is that it slows the writer down. Collecting data is very time-consuming, especially when the writer is learning the subject while gathering information. Thus this method may mean using more writers and increasing production costs.

Another drawback is that some departments may resent having an outsider come into their area to gather information. They may feel that they are being spied upon or that other people are not qualified to write about their area. The data collector/writer should be alerted to this possibility. An open, responsive, nonauthoritarian attitude can do much to defuse any hostility. It also helps to have one or two people in the user department check all data. This clearly indicates that the users are the "authorities" and ensures that the data collector/writer does not omit any vital information.

Now let's look at the second approach—having members of the user departments collect the data. The main advantage to this method is that users become actively involved in the preparation process. As a result, they feel that the manual is theirs—not something handed down from the "ivory tower"—and they are more likely to use it.

Although this approach saves the writer considerable "legwork," it may also complicate the writing process. Often user departments do not collect data in a form that is readily understandable to the writer. They assume background knowledge which the writer does not have and supply inadequate information. And because they are inexperienced at data collection, they often do not organize the material well. Consequently, the writer has to do some extensive editing and organizing before beginning to write.

Another problem is that the user departments may be too busy to give data collection high priority. They may view it as an "extra" responsibility to be completed in their spare time. And it's hard to blame them for this attitude. After all, their primary responsibility is to "get the work out," not to help prepare manuals.

As you can see, both methods have their disadvantages. The best solution, if resources permit, is to have the writer collect the data by working very closely with the user departments. If the writer does not have time to collect the data, he or she should specify the types of information needed. The user departments should supply that information and possibly even prepare the first draft. The more information the writer provides about the types of data needed, the more successful the manual will be.

RESOLVING DATA COLLECTION PROBLEMS

Data collection is fraught with potential problems. Regardless of an organization's size or the types of manuals it produces, the problems in data collection are basically the same. You're dealing with a wide range of people of varying degrees of motivation and knowledge. Corporate rivalries that you are completely unaware of may complicate the situation and create an impasse.

A common dilemma occurs when two or more sources provide conflicting information. Naturally all sources assure you that their information is completely correct. The best way to handle this problem is to explain tactfully to each person that you're perplexed by some of the data you've received and would like to arrange a meeting to clear up the confusion. At the meeting, adopt the role of mediator or arbitrator. Often the differences will be superficial or the result of poor communication. Such differences can be easily resolved.

When the conflict is more substantial, determine if the subject must be included in the manual. If it should be and if the parties involved cannot reach agreement, ask a higher authority to resolve the issue. Give the higher-ranking source an impartial statement of both sides of the conflict. Only if you have the authority to make a decision on the issue, should you do so; otherwise, remain impartial.

A second problem is that sources often provide inaccurate information. If you are sure the information is inaccurate, contact the source, explain that there appears to be a discrepancy, and ask if you can meet to resolve the problem. If the meeting is not successful, refer the situation to the appropriate authority.

Actually, determining whether the information is accurate is not normally your responsibility. All data should be either supplied or reviewed by people who are knowledgeable about the subject and who have the authority to make decisions on policies or procedures. Don't allow yourself to be placed in the position of having to make decisions in areas where you lack responsibility.

Another common problem is that employees may be reluctant to provide information. An employee may fear that in sharing knowledge with others in the organization, he or she will become expendable. Or the employee may simply be resistant to change. The employee thinks, "We've always gotten along without a manual. Why do we need one now?" Sometimes the employee is overworked and does not want to take the time to provide the necessary information. To resolve this problem, you must first determine why the employee is reluctant to provide information. If the employee is afraid of becoming expendable, he or she needs to be reassured that this is not the case. Usually the employee's supervisor or a higher-ranking manager is the appropriate person to provide reassurance. Even then, of course, the employee may not be willing to talk. In one major corporation an employee with over 20 years of experience in the tax department refused to help with a manual for fear of no longer being indispensable. Reassurance by top management did not help. This type of situation requires a direct order to "cooperate or else" from upper management. In most cases the employees will cooperate. If not, the organization is better off losing the employee now than a few years hence when he or she has become even more "indispensable."

If the employee's reluctance stems from a resistance to change, explain why the manual is needed and try to sell the employee on the idea. Point out that the manual will primarily document existing policies and procedures, not develop new ones. And if the manual is needed to comply with the requirements of regulatory agencies, tell the employee so. After all, few of us *like* to comply with the Internal Revenue Service, but virtually all of us recognize that compliance is preferable to fines or jail. If this approach does not resolve the problem, discuss it with the employee's supervisor.

If the employee's reluctance stems from a feeling of being overworked, find out if there are any other people in the department who might be able to supply the data. If not, be as cooperative and flexible as possible in scheduling the data collection. But be persistent as well. Otherwise the employee may feel that if he or she stalls long enough, you'll give up.

A final common problem in data collection is corporate politics. One department head may imply to his or her people that they should not cooperate with staff members from another department. If you encounter this situation, try to work around it by gathering information "unofficially." Here your personal contacts and relationships are your biggest asset. If you can't obtain unofficial assistance, discuss the situation with your boss and determine jointly what action is appropriate.

ORGANIZING THE DATA IN A WORKING OUTLINE

After you've collected all the data, your next step is to organize it logically by developing a working outline. If you have any grammar school phobias about outlining, put them out of your head. This type of outline is designed to help you, not to please a teacher, and the very word "working" indicates the outline's flexibility and practicality. Your outline is not carved in stone; it will undoubtedly change as the manual progresses. At the same time, it will ensure that you develop a logical organizational structure.

Guidelines for Outlining

The following guidelines will help you create a logical, comprehensive outline that will greatly simplify the writing process.

1. *Allow ample time for outlining.* Don't automatically follow the first outline you produce. Do several drafts. Outline the material in several ways, analyze each outline carefully, and then select the best one. It's much easier to correct a structural defect at the outline stage than at a more advanced phase of the writing process. And the more thoroughly you outline the manual, the simpler the remainder of the production process will be.

2. *Prepare the outline before you begin to write.* Unlike high school—where it was common practice to write a paper first and then outline it—you need to build a structure before you write. Develop your outline skeleton first. Only when it is perfected should you begin to write.

3. *Include at least two structural levels in the outline.* If you're using a traditional outline format, the two levels would be Roman numerals (I, II, III) for the main topics and capital letters (A, B, C) for the subtopics. Or you may prefer to think of the two levels as the section headings and the subtopics under each section. If you develop only one level, your outline will be too vague. Depending on the subject, you may even want a third level, using Arabic numerals (1, 2, 3). When an outline is this detailed, writing the manual is

relatively easy, since all the major organizational decisions have been made.

4. *Develop your main level of ideas first.* After you've listed all your main topics or section headings in logical order, develop appropriate subtopics for each. As you do this, you may need to alter some of the main headings to encompass a broader or narrower range of topics.

5. *Use descriptive headings.* When outlining, you'll find it tempting to use broad topic headings like "Customer Complaints." However, such catchall headings don't force you to become specific in your thoughts. A descriptive heading like "How to Handle Customer Complaints" explains exactly what aspect of the topic you will be discussing.

6. *Arrange the headings in a logical order.* Manuals are generally organized in one of three ways: functional order, process order, or descending order.

In the functional outline, ideas are grouped only by subject. All subjects are ranked equally, and there is no reason (other than alphabetical order) for placing one subject before another. For example, a functional outline for a policy manual might include such main topics as accounting, administration, manufacturing, marketing, personnel, and research and development.

A process outline is what the name implies: a listing of topics in the order in which they take place. This type of outline is normally used for individual procedures, but it can also be effective for the entire manual. This book follows the process outline form: it describes the "chronological" process of developing a manual, beginning with the planning phase and ending with revising and updating the manual. A process order sales manual might begin with a section on prospecting for leads and conclude with a section on following through on completed sales.

The descending-order outline begins with the most important subjects and ends with the least important. This structure is common in journalism. News articles begin with the most important feature of the story. Less significant details are placed at the end, where they can easily be edited out. An employee handbook written in the descending order might begin with major items such as salary administration and benefits and end with less important items such as rules concerning the company cafeteria and parking lot. When structuring an outline in descending order, you may find that some items are equally important. If this happens, don't agonize over which topic to put first; just pick one arbitrarily.

These three organizational formats—functional, process, and descending order—are not mutually exclusive. You may decide that your main headings work best in a functional manner while the items under each heading are best grouped in process order. Or your main headings might be in descending order and your subheadings functional. Just use sound judgment and common sense in selecting the organizational style(s) that seem most appropriate for your manual.

Outlining as a Review Technique

In addition to its organizational value, outlining is one of the most important review resources you have. By having your outline approved before you begin to write, you can uncover any structural problems early in the process and add or delete topics as needed. The preliminary review ensures that you and the reviewers agree on the topics to be covered and the general organization of the manual. Without such a review, you may find yourself rewriting much of the manual because a reviewer does not agree with your organizational structure or choice of topics.

CHAPTER 4

Format and Layout: Two Ways to Increase Readability

ONCE THE INFORMATION for the manual has been collected and organized, you need to spend some time planning the appearance of the manual.

Appearance is of critical importance to a successful manual. Think for a minute which you are more likely to read: a page with wide margins, ample white space, and large, clean type or a page that is covered with small type and has virtually no margins. You'd pick the well-designed, easy-to-read page—and your manual's users would make the same decision. In fact, poor design and layout are one of the main reasons that many very informative manuals remain unused.

In this chapter, we'll examine the critical areas of format and layout and discuss how to enhance your manual's physical appearance. Here, format refers to the organizational numbering (or lettering) system of the manual. Thus a format number is the numeric or alphanumeric reference assigned to each policy or procedure. Layout refers to the physical arrangement of copy on the page.

FORMAT

Although there are almost as many different formats as there are manuals, all fall into one of two categories: numeric (sometimes known as decimal) and alphanumeric.

The Numeric, or Decimal, System

As the name implies, a numeric system is based only on numbers. Decimal points, hyphens, or blank spaces are used to separate the groupings of numbers. Numeric systems are the most commonly used format for manuals. Some systems are extremely effective; others are so complex as to be virtually useless. The most frequently used numeric formats are:

00 00 or 00–00 or 00.00   With this two-level system, the first two-digit number represents a section in the manual, and the second two-digit number designates a particular policy, procedure, or other document within that section. The numbers may be staggered rather than assigned consecutively so as to allow room for expansion within the section or to permit the insertion of new sections. For example, the section numbers might be 10, 20, 30 and so on rather than 01, 02, 03, and so on. This system allows you to insert additional sections such as 15 between 10 and 20.

00 00 00 or 00–00–00 or 00.00.00   This three-level system is similar to the preceding two-level system. However, the extra level permits additional subdividing within a section. The first two digits usually represent a major section, the second two indicate a subsection, and the final two represent the individual policy, procedure, or document.

000–00   Here each digit in the first three-digit grouping has a separate meaning. The first represents a major section or a division of the organization, the second is a subsection or department, and the third indicates a further organizational (or sub-subsectional) breakdown. The final two-digit grouping represents the policy, procedure, or other document.

0.0000 or 0.0.0.0.0   This rather awkward system is the traditional decimal format, used frequently by government groups. At times, it has even more than the five levels shown here. With this system, a relatively few main sections are broken down into increasingly smaller parts, with each digit or decimal point and digit representing a further subdivision. Because of the elaborate subdivisions, this system confuses many readers and should be avoided if possible.

The above list is not all-inclusive, of course—there are almost as many possible formats as there are manuals. However, the list suggests the range of possibilities, and with the exception of the traditional decimal system (0.0000 or 0.0.0.0.0), all the numeric formats discussed above are effective for manuals.

The Alphanumeric System

As the name implies, alphanumeric formats use both letters and numbers. They generally fall into one of two categories. The first type is the traditional outline format: I.A.1.a.

Here the first level (roman numeral) represents the main section or chapter heading. The second level (capital letter) is a subsection. The third (arabic numeral) and fourth (lowercase letter) levels allow for further subject division. Because of its relative inflexibility, this format should not be used if extensive structural changes or additions are expected.

This system is the preferred method for presenting the text within an individual policy or procedure. For example, on a specific policy, roman numeral I might be "Purpose," II might be "Responsibility," and III might be "Policy." Underneath each heading the text would be broken down into A, B, C, and under these into 1, 2, 3, and so on, as needed. Most users are very comfortable with this format, since it is commonly found in outlines and other contexts.

One caution—because roman numerals are used less frequently now than in the past, users do not realize what numbers the higher roman numerals (IX and above) represent. One way to avoid confusion is to use, A, B, C as the first level; 1, 2, 3 as the second; a, b, c as the third, and so on.

The second type of alphanumeric system uses letter codes to indicate the department or section and numbers to indicate the specific policy, procedure, or other document. This extremely simple, effective system is very popular with users because letter codes are much easier to remember than numbers. Some common examples of this system are:

ACC 00	Accounting document number 00
LEG 00	Legal document number 00
PER 00	Personnel document number 00

Obviously, it's easier to remember that ACC represents "Accounting" than that section 01 is "Accounting." And with this system new sections can be inserted in the correct alphabetic position without affecting other sections.

As with the numeric formats, the alphanumeric systems have many variations. Although these systems are somewhat less flexible than numeric formats, they are generally preferred by users.

Guidelines for Developing an Effective Format

At this point, developing a format may seem frustrating because of the variety of choices and the lack of hard-and-fast rules. No one format is clearly superior to all others. Your task as preparer is to evaluate all possible formats and select the one that is best suited to the material and easiest for the user to understand. The following guidelines will help you accomplish that objective.

1. *You should normally limit your overall format to three levels.* Four is the absolute maximum. A three-level system includes sections, subsections, and individual policies, procedures, or topics. The more levels there are, the greater the chance of confusing the reader. Users may forget the relationship between the levels or may have difficulty finding the desired information. These problems occur most frequently with the traditional decimal system (1.1.1.1.1.), which usually has five to seven levels.

If you find that a section has over three levels, try breaking the first and second levels down into more specific main headings. For example, you might change the section heading "Employment Practices" to more precise headings such as "Hiring," "Termination," and "Attendance" instead of using these titles for subsections. By eliminating one whole format level, you give the user simple, specific section headings instead of vague, catchall titles.

2. *Remember that most people find an alphanumeric system more readable than a numeric system.* In other words, most people relate better to letters than to numbers. However, if a simple numeric system appears to work best for your material, don't hesitate to use it.

3. *Develop more than one possible format, and survey users to determine their preferences.* All too often, extremely complex formats are developed for the convenience of the manual's preparers, and users are forced to cope with a system that is not designed for them. Field testing helps you avoid complex, unworkable formats and lets the users participate in the decision. Consequently, users are more likely to accept the new system.

4. *If possible, use the same type of format for all manuals in the organization.* When each manual has a different format, users never really learn any of the systems and are continually disoriented. When each manual has the same format, users quickly become accustomed to it—and the format encourages, rather than discourages, use of the manual.

5. *Explain the format in the introductory section of the manual.* The "how to use this manual" portion of the introduction should explain exactly how the format works and give examples. (Chapter 6 examines the manual's introduction in detail.)

6. *If your organization's manuals have a workable existing format, continue to use it.* Frequently a format is quite understandable and adequate for the material, but somewhat confusing to the new user. However, the format has been in existence for many years and is an old friend to most of the manual's users. In this type of situation, it is best not to alter the manual's format. It's easier for the occasional new user to learn the old system than for everyone in the organization to adapt to a new system.

If you're not sure whether the existing format is effective, conduct a user survey. Don't confine your questions to whether the users like the format; find out if they understand it. Ask them what the various letters or numbers mean. And ask if they would prefer to keep the existing format or switch to a new one. Give them two or three choices for a new format and explain each, with examples.

PAGE NUMBERING

After you've selected a format, your next task is to decide how to number the pages. And *do* number them. It is unbelievably frustrating to work with an unnumbered manual. Just try referring people to the eighth (or, worse yet, the twentieth) page from the beginning of a section and watch them count pages until they reach the right one. The lack of pagination is an enormous demotivator.

There are three basic page-numbering systems for manuals. The manual's format, content, and frequency of revision determine which system is most appropriate.

Consecutive page numbering is the simplest system for the user, but it's also the least flexible. With this system, each page is numbered in order, beginning with 1. This system is feasible only when the manual is bound in book form, not in a binder, and when no revisions or updates will be made. Instead, the manual is reprinted periodically with corrections. For example, with employee handbooks and other high-distribution manuals, changes are infrequent and printing the manual as a booklet is often more cost-effective.

Section page numbering is also fairly simple to understand, but like consecutive numbering it lacks flexibility. With sectional numbering, the pages in a section are numbered consecutively and each page number is preceded by the section number and a hyphen. For example:

> 1-12   (page 12 of section 1)
> 2-1   (page 1 of section 2)

This system is fine if pages will be added or deleted only at the end of a section rather than in the middle. However, relatively few manuals meet that requirement. If yours does, use sectional numbering. For the rare addition not at the section's end, add lowercase letters to the preceding page number (2-12, 2-12a, 2-12b). Do not overuse this technique, however, or the pagination will become confusing.

Document page numbering is the third pagination system for manuals. With this system, each policy, procedure, or other document is paged individually. If policy 12-05 has three pages, they are numbered 1, 2, and 3. The user first locates the policy or procedure through the format numbering system and then finds the desired page within the document. Although document numbering is a somewhat more complex system for the user, it has the flexibility needed by the preparer of the manual. Revisions and deletions require only a change in the page numbers of the individual policy or procedure and do not affect any other portion of the manual.

To indicate the page number in the document numbering system, some manual preparers add a hyphen and page number to the format number at the top of each page. Thus, 12-05-1 means page 1 of policy 12-05. This approach makes the format appear more complex than it actually is and can confuse the user. For that reason, I prefer to list the page number separately from the format number (12-05, page 1). Other examples of this style appear later in the chapter under the discussion of standard page headings.

Some organizations not only list the page numbers separately from the format numbers, but state "page 1 of 2," "page 2 of 4," and so on, to indicate how many pages are in the entire document. The rationale is that users can easily determine if they have the complete document. If losing pages is a problem or if users cannot easily determine if a page is missing, you may want to adopt this system. However, it is generally unnecessary and expensive: when material is added to the document, the entire document must be reprinted to correct the page numbering.

LAYOUT

As mentioned earlier, layout refers to the way the copy is arranged on the page. An attractive layout not only improves the manual's physical appearance; it also increases its readability. This section gives some general guidelines for designing an attractive layout for a manual.

1. *Use "white space" effectively.* White space is the printing term for the areas on a page where there is no type. Don't economize on paper by keeping white space to a minimum; the generous and logical use of white space will make the manual much more read-

able. Think of placing your copy on the page the same way you position a painting on a wall to enhance its effect.

2. *Leave ample margins.* This is a corollary to the first guideline. Leave between 1⅛″ to 1⅜″ margins on the top, bottom, and sides of the page. It's very frustrating to read a manual with holes punched into the text and copy practically running off the sides and bottom of the page. Wide margins make the pages more attractive and easier to read.

3. *Do not indent paragraphs.* Instead, leave extra white space between paragraphs or items in a list. Use white space to group your ideas as well as to make the page more visually appealing. For example, if you single-space the copy in a paragraph, double-space between paragraphs. A page with the single-space, double-space combination is easier to read than a page with all double-spacing.

4. *Use block indentation at each level of the text.* Doing this ensures that the numbers and letters identifying each item are not obscured. In the following example of block indentation, the x's represent the text.

     1. xxxxxxxxxxxxxxxxxxxxxxxxxxxxxxxxxxxxxxxxxx
         xxxxxxxxxxxxxxxxxxxxxxxxxxxxxxxxxxxxxxxxxx

       a.   xxxxxxxxxxxxxxxxxxxxxxxxxxxxxxxxxxxxxxxxxx
           xxxxxxxxxxxxxxxxxxxxxxxxxxxxxxxxxxxxxxxxxx

Without block indentation, the "1" and the "a" would be hidden as in this example:

     1. xxxxxxxxxxxxxxxxxxxxxxxxxxxxxxxxxxxxxxxxxx
xxxxxxxxxxxxxxxxxxxxxxxxxxxxxxxxxxxxxxxxxxxx

       a.   xxxxxxxxxxxxxxxxxxxxxxxxxxxxxxxxxxxxxxxxxx
xxxxxxxxxxxxxxxxxxxxxxxxxxxxxxxxxxxxxxxxxxxx

Or worse yet:

       b.   xxxxxxxxxxxxxxxxxxxxxxxxxxxxxxxxxxxxxx
xxxxxxxxxxxxxxxxxxxxxxxxxxxxxxxxxxxxxxxxxxxx

And, as you can see, block indents make the page look more attractive.

5. *Do not exceed 65 characters per line.* This is the longest line length the eye can scan comfortably. If you are using generous margins, following this rule should come naturally.

6. *Use "ragged right" margins.* Ragged right margins are margins that are not justified or aligned on the right side. Studies show that copy with ragged right margins is easier to read, partly because fewer words are hyphenated and no unnaturally wide spaces occur between words.

If you are reproducing typed copy for your manual and do not have word processing, ragged right copy is inevitable. In fact, your typists would probably mutiny if you asked them to justify each line manually. If you have the capability to justify lines through word processing or typesetting, don't use it. This is one instance where a technological advance is not necessarily an improvement.

7. *Use a clean readable typeface.* Most standard typewriter typefaces are quite acceptable for manuals. However, manuals typed in script (italics) are virtually unreadable. If possible, use a serif typeface, not a sans-serif one, especially if the manual is typeset. Serifs are short lines stemming from and at an angle to the upper and lower ends of a letter. (This book is set in Baskerville type, a serif style.) A sans-serif type does not have serifs and can be used effectively in headings. (The display headings in this book are set in Helvetica, a sans-serif type.) However, in large blocks of copy, sans-serif type becomes monotonous and difficult to read. In fact, research shows that most people can read 5 to 21 words per minute with a serif type than with a sans-serif type. For this reason, most books and magazines are set in serif type.

8. *Avoid fine print.* Some organizations have their manuals printed in infinitesimal type. The rationale here is that you can fit more copy on a page. Yes, you can, but users can't read it easily and tend to not read it at all. To achieve this effect, a standard pica (10 characters to the inch) or elite (12 characters to the inch) typeface is reduced photographically. The reduction decreases readability and adds another step and an additional cost to the production process. If your manual needs to go on a diet, remove the excess verbiage (see Chapter 7) instead of shrinking the type.

If you have a choice between pica and elite type, use the pica, which is larger and slightly easier to read.

STANDARD PAGE HEADINGS

A standard page heading is a specially marked-off area at the top of each page which contains certain basic information, such as the title of the manual, the title of the policy, procedure, or other document, the format and page numbers, and the date issued. Standard headings consolidate a great deal of information in a relatively small space and provide the user with a quick reference. They are most frequently used in policy and procedure manuals.

No one standard heading is superior to all others. In fact, this is one area where you can bring your creative skills into play. Here are some guidelines for developing standard page headings. (Samples are shown at the end of this section.)

1. *Include only necessary information.* Do not pack the heading with an enormous amount of detail that is of little or no interest to the user. If you are unsure whether to include an item, ask yourself, "Does the user really need to know this, or am I including it for my own convenience?"

The following list of items frequently included in headings is presented cafeteria style. Select only those items appropriate for your manual.

Company logo
Title of manual
Title of policy, procedure, or other document
Format number
Page number
Department issuing the document
Applicability (if a policy or procedure is applicable only to a certain
    group of users—for example, employees at the Broadview office)
Date issued or date effective

2. *Don't print names or people's signatures.* Users do not need to know that Samantha Smith wrote the procedure. Nor do they need to see the signatures of several top management personnel to know that this is an official policy that must be followed. Including names or signatures only gratifies egos and consumes valuable space. Moreover, when one of the "signatures" leaves the organization, people may wonder whether the policy or procedure is still in effect.

Instead of signatures, include in the manual's introductory section a statement that the manual's contents have been approved by management and should be followed. Of course, keep review copies with approval signatures in your files in case a question arises about the approval. .

3. *If you include the company logo in the heading, keep it small.* The logo is an effective means of identification and takes up less space than the company name. Just don't let it dominate the page. Remember, you're preparing a manual, not an advertisement.

4. *Emphasize items according to their importance to the reader.* Usually the title of the policy or procedure is the most important item and should be prominently displayed. The title of the manual is also important. It is of value to users if a page gets separated from the manual and ensures that users place updates in the correct manual. The format and page numbers are traditionally placed on the right side.

5. *Place all information at the top of the page, rather than some at the top and some at the bottom.* Then the user need only look in one place. Also, information at the bottom of the page is often overlooked, especially if the text does not completely fill the page.

6. *Don't block off the entire page with lines.* Some designers of manuals extend the heading lines down the sides of the page and across the bottom. Like Agatha Christie's detective, Hercule Poiròt, these designers believe in perfect symmetry—in this case, a geometrically elegant page. The problem is that the lines cut off the margins, and the text appears imprisoned in a tight box. The result is decreased readability.

7. *Keep the heading simple and tasteful.* Less is better than more. A simple, clean heading with only essential information is the ideal. Your heading should not overwhelm or detract from the text on the page.

8. *Consider printing the standard heading in color for a more professional look.* Since the blank sheets with heading forms are all printed at once, the additional cost for using colored ink instead of black usually is minimal. Color gives the pages a distinctive, professional look and makes the manual look more attractive. However, printing the heading form in two colors, even if one is black, will mean two press runs and will double your printing costs for the heading sheets.

9. *For multiple-page policies or procedures, either use the same heading for all pages or design a simpler heading for page 2, page 3, and so on.* If the initial page heading is simple and well designed, it can be used for all pages, saving you the time and expense of preparing a second heading. If you are printing the manual on both sides of the paper, do not reverse the page heading for the back side. Reversing the heading is visually distracting and often confuses the user. Instead, simply repeat the heading on the reverse side.

Figure 3 shows three sample headings. The information given on each varies, but all occupy a relatively small portion of the page and can be prepared easily in-house with a minimum of expense.

Figure 3. Sample page headings.

LO GO	POLICY MANUAL	TITLE Affirmative Action Policy		NO. P-02
		DEPT. ISSUING Personnel	DATE ISSUED 2/28/80 R	PAGE 1

LO GO	ACCOUNTING PROCEDURES MANUAL		NO. 03-09
SUBJECT Adding a new account to the general ledger		DATE ISSUED 2/28/80	PAGE 2

LO GO	PERSONNEL POLICY/PROCEDURES		SECTION Employee Benefits	
TITLE Short-Term Disability		DATE EFFECT. 3/1/80	NO. 40-05	PAGE 1

CHAPTER 5

Selecting Binders, Index Tabs, and Paper

THIS CHAPTER deals with the most cosmetic aspect of preparing a manual: selecting its binder, index tabs, and paper. You can spend a great deal of money or relatively little on each item, and the amount spent does not necessarily relate directly to the item's effectiveness. Some expensively produced manuals end up being attractive dust collectors. Other manuals with inexpensive but functional binders, tabs, and paper are extremely successful. Clearly, cost is not the most important criterion.

BINDERS

Selecting a functional, attractive, yet economical binder can present a real dilemma to the novice. Usually the only sources of information on binders are the binder sales representative, who is hardly unbiased, and the corporate purchasing agent, who is often unaware of the special qualities needed for a binder used for a manual. Here are some tips on selecting the right binder for your manual.

Binder Size

A common error is ordering the largest binder available—a monster that will accommodate reams of paper. The problem here is that users are going to have difficulty pulling the binder off the shelf, not to mention using it. Generally, a 2½″ binder (2½″ refers to the size of the ring, not the width of the spine) is the maximum desirable size. If you have too much material to fit in that size binder, use two binders.

Since manuals, like children, tend to grow rapidly, it's a good idea to start with a binder that's slightly over half full. Then you'll have ample room for growth—but the manual will not look ridiculously empty at the start.

Types of Binders

Let's begin with a "don't." Don't use a flexible vinyl binder (one piece of heavy vinyl bent around a ring spine). These binders are less expensive than rigid vinyl binders (ones with vinyl-covered cardboard fronts, backs, and spines), but economy is their only advantage. The flexible binders don't stand up on bookshelves, and with frequent use they crack at the spine. Also, the rings can press through the cover, damaging both binder and spine.

For most manuals, a three-ring binder is preferable. Although seven-ring binders protect the paper better from wear, they cost more and tend to discourage users from updating the manual. And, by all means, avoid monstrosities such as 18- or 25-ring binders. These are extremely expensive, and they make updating even more frustrating to the user.

If you have a great deal of material to include in the manual, you should consider using a D-ring binder. These binders will hold up to 25 percent more paper than a comparably sized standard round-ring binder. Since the straight and slanted D-rings (see Figure 4) are mounted on the back cover of the binder instead of the spine, the binder always lies flat and the paper does not move when the binder is opened. Consequently, there is less strain on the paper and pages do not tear out as easily.

D-ring binders are more expensive than standard round-ring binders, but most organizations find the additional expense well worth it. Some users complain that it is difficult to insert and re-

Figure 4. Ring binders.

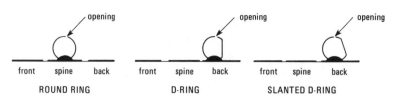

move paper when the binder is full. The slight pitch to the right side of the slanted D-ring reduces that problem.

One last bit of advice—don't be afraid to be different. Just because the standard three-ring binder is ideal for most manuals does not mean it is the best choice for yours. Consider all alternatives before making a decision.

For manuals used by computer terminal operators, easel binders (ones that stand up) are extremely effective. An operator can stand the binder beside the terminal and look from the binder to the screen without refocusing his or her gaze.

Another approach is to print all overall corporate policies in a bound 4″ × 6″ booklet. At least one large manufacturing company has found it cheaper to publish policies in booklet form and to reprint the booklet with changes (usually once a year) than to supply everyone with a binder. Also, they no longer have to worry about users keeping their manuals up to date.

The booklet format is also advantageous for employee handbooks, which have a large distribution and are updated relatively infrequently. Manuals for railroad and trucking industry personnel are frequently printed as booklets because the users must keep the manuals with them on the job and binders are simply too bulky.

Binder Design

In designing a binder cover your creativity and the amount of money you have to spend are the only limits. I've seen binder covers that could hang in a museum and others that would win no design awards but that were totally functional and economical. The direction you choose is up to you. In either case, there are some practical pointers you should keep in mind.

Avoid light-colored vinyl, which picks up dirt easily. I learned this the hard way when I chose some light gray binders that quickly picked up black smudges and fingerprints. In the salesperson's samples, lighter colors often seem more attractive or impressive than dark ones, but don't make this common mistake.

Print the manual's name on the spine as well as on the front cover so it can be identified easily on the bookshelf. And have the name printed horizontally rather than vertically for greater readability. (See Figure 5.) The title on the spine should be in full caps, not upper and lower case. Again, this is for ease of reading.

Figure 5. Positioning title on spine.

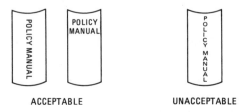

ACCEPTABLE   UNACCEPTABLE

An economical, yet attractive approach to binder design is to use a binder with clear or translucent vinyl pockets covering the entire spine and front cover. Inserts identifying the manual can be printed on card stock and placed in the pockets. The result is a manual that looks custom-designed but that is much less expensive than silk screening, which is a process of printing on vinyl or cloth. And if you order binders with a vinyl pocket on the back cover as well, you can use light colors.

Because binders with vinyl pockets can be used throughout the organization for a variety of purposes, they can be ordered at quantity discounts. Also, they are reusable. One final note: translucent vinyl is preferable for the cover pockets because it resists scratching better than clear vinyl.

If economy is a critical factor, order standard three-ring binders with a metal pocket on the spine for the title. These relatively inexpensive binders are quite functional, if not glamorous.

Ordering and Shipping Binders

Order your binders well in advance. It often takes six to eight weeks to have an order filled, especially if the covers are being silk-screened. Stock binders with vinyl pockets can usually be shipped more quickly.

Some binder sales representatives will blithely promise unrealistic delivery dates to get your order. Try to find a salesperson who has served your organization (or other organizations you know) satisfactorily in the past.

Do not order binders with pockets on the inside front or back covers. Not only do these pockets cost more, but they tempt users to file updates in the pockets rather than place them in the binders.

If your binders will be shipped in extremely cold weather, make sure they are allowed to warm up in their cartons before they are unpacked. Otherwise, the vinyl may crack. Even the highest grade of vinyl—Grade D, Class 120—will crack at $-20°F$, and the lowest grade—Grade A, Class 90—will crack at $+10°F$. Even if your binders will not face temperature extremes, it is advisable to order Grade D vinyl for its increased durability.

Never ship a binder with the pages already inserted in the rings. The pages will tear and the rings may be damaged. Instead, shrink-wrap the pages in clear plastic wrap which is heat-sealed or band them together with a paper strip; then place them in the binder but not in the rings. Users can insert the pages in the rings when they receive the binders.

INDEX TABS

Selecting index tabs is much less complicated than selecting binders. The most important factor is that the tabs should be sturdy enough to last the life of the manual. Since they are unlikely to change when the manual is updated, it's worthwhile to spend a little more and get tabs that can hold up under heavy use.

No matter what type of tab you select, have both the section title and format number printed on both sides. Then users will have no difficulty finding a desired section if they flip through the manual from the back to the front. Stock tabs with numbers only are less expensive, but they are of little value to the user. Very few people remember that section 3 is accounting and section 4 is administration.

For maximum readability, the items on the tabs should be printed in full caps and the numbers should be printed in the same direction as the section name, not perpendicular to it (see Figure 6). Have both tabs and holes reinforced with Mylar for durability. Reinforcement substantially increases the life span of the tabs and

Figure 6. Positioning information on index tabs.

ACCEPTABLE   UNACCEPTABLE

is well worth the additional expense. Mylar is preferable to acetate because it is stronger and thinner. If you use colored tabs, remember that dark shades obscure the printing on the tabs. Dark greens, blues, and reds are especially bad in this respect.

If you have extremely long sections (more than 75 pages), use smaller tabs to mark off major subsections so that the user will not have difficulty locating material. Tabs for subsections should not be as wide as the section tabs so that the two can be easily distinguished. And if you are tabbing both sections and subsections, use one color for the section tabs and another for the subsections.

Just as you can "undertab" a manual, so you can "overtab" it. If your manual has a multitude of five-page sections, restructure it so it has fewer and more substantial main headings.

PAPER

Selecting paper is a relatively simple decision. However, it can lead to disaster if you ignore a few simple rules.

First use a standard paper stock that will be readily available in the future. Consult with your purchasing agent or printer about an appropriate choice. I remember well a training manual I had printed on an expensive textured stock. The manual looked very impressive until we had to begin adding updates on a standard bond paper because the textured stock was no longer available.

If you plan to print your manual on both sides of the page, select a paper that is heavy enough to prevent "bleed-through." Bleed-through is the printer's term for type that shows through on the reverse side of the page. Bleed-through is distracting and makes reading quite difficult.

With the proper weight of paper, printing on both sides is an excellent idea; it reduces paper costs and makes the manual less bulky. Do, however, begin each policy, procedure, or subject on a separate page so that updating will not become a problem.

Some organizations use paper with Mylar-backed holes. Such paper is extremely costly and makes the manual more bulky. Normally, it's also unnecessary, except possibly for the title page and sheets that receive extremely heavy use. It is the tabs that receive the most strain, not the paper. And because the paper is usually replaced frequently with updates, it rarely tears out.

Use colored paper only if you have a good reason. I remember one manual that was a veritable rainbow of color. I went through it carefully and could not determine why some pages were blue, some green, and so on. When I asked, I was told that the print shop had wanted to use up some odd lots of leftover paper. Obviously, that is not a good reason for using color.

However, color can be used intelligently and effectively to distinguish between different types of documents. For example, all policies might be printed on one color of paper and all procedures on another. Or interim policies or procedures might be printed on colored stock to differentiate them from the permanent versions.

If you use color, pick shades that are easy on the reader's eye, such as pale green and pale yellow. Blue paper can cause eyestrain, because black type does not stand out clearly on it. Also, test the colors you choose to see how well they photocopy. Blue, in particular, does not photocopy well. This may or may not be a disadvantage. Some organizations use blue paper precisely because they do not want people to photocopy the manual.

Finally, be sure to select standard shades that will continue to be available. Otherwise, you may end up with five or six variations of one color in your manual.

CHAPTER 6

Introducing Users to the Manual

EVERY MANUAL should have an introductory section that gives the user an overview of the manual, explains how to use it, and tells where everything is located. The opening section accomplishes these objectives through (1) a table of contents, (2) an index, and (3) an introduction. Without such a section, the user must play detective, attempting to decipher the format and find the needed information.

Before we proceed, let's define some terms. A table of contents and an index are not synonymous. A table of contents is a sequential listing of the items included in the manual. Topics are listed in the order in which they appear. An index is an alphabetical listing of the subjects discussed in the manual.

A manual should have both a table of contents and an index. Each serves a different purpose. The table of contents gives users an overview of the entire manual and helps them find a particular topic. In a sense it is the manual's skeleton, or framework. The index enables the user to find all references to any subject quickly. Therefore, it complements the table of contents rather than duplicating it. The two together provide the user with a complete reference system.

In a book such as this one, the index is at the end—which is where the reader expects to find it. For a manual, however, I recommend placing the index at the beginning, immediately after the table of contents. The rationale is simple. Because many manuals do not have indexes, the user does not automatically expect to find one. If the index is placed at the end of the manual, it may be overlooked. If it's at the beginning, even the most infrequent user is likely to discover it.

PREPARING THE TABLE OF CONTENTS

The table of contents should be the first item after the title page and the index tab for the introductory section. Preparing the table of contents is one of the easiest tasks in developing the manual. After all, the table of contents is really just a polished version of your outline, with format number references added. Here are some guidelines for developing an effective table of contents for the manual.

1. *Go into detail.* A table of contents should not just list the section headings; it should also include the items or topics in each section. If these items are omitted, the user has to play a frustrating game of guessing which topics are included in each section.

2. *Give the appropriate numeric or alphanumeric reference for each item in the table of contents.* Also include the page number if you're using a consecutive or sectional page numbering system.

3. *Use white space, indenting, and/or capitalization to indicate the relationship of the items listed in table.* The sample tables of contents in Figure 7 illustrate some different ways of arranging the material on the page. You should use white space generously so the user can find items in the table easily.

4. *Place format references to the left of the items listed.* This technique makes it easier for the user to link items and their reference numbers and eliminates the need for leaders (long lines of dots connecting items and numbers). If you include page numbers as well, put them in their traditional position at the right. They are not important enough to take precedence over the titles.

Some organizations include the latest revision date of every item in the table of contents. This increases the updating expense, since the table must be revised every time the manual is updated. Organizations that use this approach argue that it's easy to tell if the manual is up to date by checking the table of contents. Actually, if users are not updating the body of the manual, they are highly unlikely to be updating the table of contents either.

Figure 7. Sample tables of contents.

Sample 1

   10-00 INTRODUCTION

   10-01 Table of contents
   10-02 Index
   10-03 How to use this manual

   20-00 ACCOUNTING

   20-01 Account codes
   20-02 Establishing or changing accounts

Sample 2

   Title   *Page*

Title	Page
1. INTRODUCTION	
A. Table of contents	1-1
B. Index	1-3
C. How to use this manual	1-7
2. ACCOUNTING	
A. Account codes	2-1
B. Establishing or changing accounts	2-5

---

5. *Use "mini" tables of contents to assist your users.* A "mini" table of contents lists all the items in a particular section and is placed at the beginning of that section. It does not replace the complete table of contents at the beginning of the manual, but it is a handy reference for the user.

Do not print the section table of contents on the face of the index tab for that section. When you have changes in the table, as you inevitably will, you will have to reprint the tab—which is much more costly than reprinting a sheet of paper. Also users rarely look at the front of a tab; they open the book with the tab on the left side and the first page of the section on the right (another reason for printing the section name on both sides of the index tab).

PREPARING THE INDEX

As noted earlier, the index is an alphabetical listing of the subjects discussed in the manual. It is not simply an alphabetical listing of policy or procedure titles. After all, one policy or procedure may cover three or four key subjects, all of which should be included in the index.

Preparing an index can be very time-consuming and tedious if it must be done manually. However, if your organization has a word processing or computer system that can be programmed to develop an index, your task is relatively simple. Check for the availability of such a system in your organization. Since there are a variety of different systems in use, you will need to find out the appropriate procedure from your word processing or data processing staff.

If your manual must be indexed manually, consider hiring a professional freelance indexer. Contact publishers or communications associations in your area for leads on qualified freelancers. The saving in time and effort more than justifies the additional expenditure. If you decide to prepare your index manually in house, here's how to do it:

1. Begin indexing when you begin writing the manual. Write each topic you cover on a separate index card along with its location or approximate location in the manual. File the cards alphabetically. When a subject recurs, simply note the new location on the existing index card.
2. When the manual is ready for printing, go through the file and verify or correct all location references. Then your index can be typed directly from the cards.
3. If you're adding an index to an existing manual, go through the manual page by page and write down each topic and its location on a separate index card. File the cards alphabetically as you prepare them. The completed file is then ready to be typed.

Whether you prepare your index manually or mechanically, you should follow certain rules.

1. *List subjects under all possible names that might occur to users.* For example, you might list the policy on "sick leave" under "sick leave," "leave, sick," "absence due to illness," and "illness, absence

due to." And avoid cross-referencing in the index. Users quickly become frustrated if they look up "absence due to illness" and are told, "see sick leave." Do not, however, index items under nonkey words. I remember one manual where "handling new accounts" was indexed under "handling," not under "accounts" or "new accounts."

If you're preparing the index manually, indicate all cross-references on each subject card. Then when you update the index, you won't forget to change all listings of the subject.

2. *Test your index.* Ask some users to pick several topics they might refer to in the manual and try to find them in the index. If the users have no difficulty locating the items, your index is ready for production. If the users do have problems, revise the index accordingly. It's also a good idea to spot-check some items in the index to be sure they refer the user to the proper page.

3. *Use plenty of white space when you have the index typed.* I usually leave one to two inches between each alphabetical division. Not only does this make the index easier to read, but it ensures that you can add new items under each letter without having to reprint every page. Of course, be sure to insert the new items in their correct alphabetical position, not at the end of a letter's listings.

To save space, you may wish to have the index printed in two columns. If you do, be sure to leave generous margins and at least half an inch between the columns.

4. *Keep the index up to date.* Unless the index is revised regularly, it quickly becomes useless. Although it is impractical to print a new index or portion of an index every time the manual is revised, you should issue an updated index regularly. Quarterly index revisions are usually an effective compromise. Of course, you should update the original index rather than issue a supplement. If users have to look through the index and then through one or more supplements to find a subject, they will soon ignore the manual altogether.

PREPARING THE INTRODUCTION

In addition to a table of contents and an index, the opening section should include a brief introduction to the manual. The emphasis here is on the word "brief." If the introduction is long, rambling, and pompous, users will probably assume the entire manual is written in the same style and not read further.

In the introduction, do not describe in detail the evolution of the manual or the philosophy of the organization. Instead, quickly tell users what the manual is about, how it affects them, and how they can use it.

The precise nature of the introduction depends on the type of manual you're producing. However, you should consider including the following items:

Purpose	Describe what the organization hopes to accomplish with the manual. Keep your remarks brief and to the point; otherwise, the user will skip right over them.
Scope	Briefly explain what the manual covers: all corporate policies, the procedures followed by a particular department, or whatever. You may even want to combine the scope and the purpose in one statement.
Applicability	This is a very important item because it tells users whether or not they are affected by the manual. For example, the manual might be applicable to all managers at the company or to all employees of the accounting department.
Authority	Here's where the statement of official approval belongs, not in the standard page heading or at the end of each policy. Use titles, not names, in this section. For example, simply state that the board of directors has approved all corporate policies or that the vice president of finance has approved all accounting department procedures.

How to use this manual This section is probably the most important part of the introduction. It tells users everything they need to know to use the manual. And, hopefully, it eliminates phone calls from users who don't understand the numbering system or who want to find out the procedure for reporting an error.

The "how to use this manual" section should include:

- A brief explanation of the format.
- A statement of the users' responsibilities—for example, keeping the manual up to date and returning it to the organization if they leave.
- The department or job title to contact if users have any corrections, changes, or suggestions for the manual.
- An explanation of any special symbols or codes, such as those used to indicate revised material.
- A brief description of any special features, such as a glossary or forms section.
- A discussion of anything else the user needs to know in order to use the manual.

Introductions to Policies or Procedures

You've probably seen some of the items mentioned above used in introductions to individual policies and procedures. There's nothing wrong with this practice unless you end up with a one-page introduction to a four-line policy or a three-step procedure. Let's look at each item to determine if it belongs in an individual document.

Include a purpose or scope statement only if it does not simply duplicate the document's title. For example, there is no point stating that the purpose of a procedure entitled "opening a new account" is to teach tellers how to open a new account.

If a statement of applicability is appropriate, include it in the standard page heading rather than the body of the document. It takes up less space there and can be quickly spotted by users.

As explained in the section on standard page headings, you should omit statements of authority from individual policies or procedures. And, of course, you would not include a statement on how to use the policy or procedure.

One item that you would not include in the introduction but that you may need to include in a policy or procedure is a section titled definitions. Follow this rule of thumb: If a term is critical to understanding the document and if most users are unfamiliar with the term, define it at the beginning of the document. If most (but not all) users are familiar with the term, put it in a glossary at the end of the manual. And mention the glossary in the "how to use this manual" portion of the introduction.

CHAPTER 7

The Writing Process: Step by Step

WRITING A MANUAL is very different from writing a novel, an essay, or an article for a journal. However, certain basic rules of grammar and logic apply to all types of writing. Manuals are not literary masterpieces designed to make subtle distinctions or to display the author's erudition or poetic sensibilities. Instead, they should be direct, concise, and easy to understand. Readers should not have to interpret the material or draw conclusions; they need only do what the manual says.

Obviously, it is impossible to cover all the fundamentals of good writing in this book. Instead, this chapter will concentrate on nine principles that apply to all business writing. The remainder of the chapter deals with three writing techniques designed specifically for manuals: step-by-step listing, playscript, and action-condition logic.

PRINCIPLES OF EFFECTIVE WRITING

1. *Use the active voice.* Failure to use the active voice is the most common writing problem in manuals. First, let's distinguish between the active and passive voice. With the active voice, the subject of the sentence performs the action; with the passive voice, the subject is acted upon, or receives the action. Also, the passive voice always includes a form of the verb *to be.*

Here's an example of each voice:

Active	The accounts receivable clerk completes Form 29 for each new account. (*Active voice: the clerk performs the action.*)
Passive	Form 29 is completed for each new account.
	OR
Passive	Form 29 is completed for each new account by the accounts receivable clerk. (*Passive voice: in each case, the action is performed on Form 29*. Also, each verb includes *is,* a form of the verb *to be.*)

As you can see, the sentence written in the active voice is more direct and more vigorous and clearly indicates who does what. With the passive voice, it's easy to omit the clerk, as in the first passive example.

The primary purpose of most manuals is to tell users what their specific responsibilities are. Yet these same manuals consistently are written in the passive voice, which obscures or eliminates statements of responsibility. You're not being rude or discourteous if you tell users what to do in a direct manner, using the active voice. If you were speaking to an employee, you would say, "Write a report on your trip," not "A report should be written on your trip." Why not be equally direct in your manual?

2. *Write in the present tense whenever possible.* Another common problem in manuals is the tendency to use the future tense. The result is sentences like this:

Form 29 will be completed for each new account by the accounts receivable clerk. (*passive voice, future tense*)

OR

The accounts receivable clerk will complete Form 29 for each new account. (*active voice, future tense*)

While the second example is preferable, neither one is desirable. In both cases, the action takes place in the future, not now. And the purpose of a manual is to get results now. Also, writing in the future tense makes sentences longer. Remember: "will" is usually an unnecessary word in manuals.

3. *Omit needless words.* Good writing is concise; every word serves

a purpose and cannot be omitted without altering the sentence's meaning. Unfortunately, this rule is often ignored in business writing. Unnecessary or redundant words and phrases are used in the belief that these expressions are more professional or business-like.

Here is a list of deadwood expressions frequently found in manuals and other business writing.

DEADWOOD	REPLACEMENT
according to our records	*(either omit or cite a specific source)*
actually	*(usually omit)*
at the present time	now
attached hereto	attached
basic essentials	essentials
cooperate together	cooperate
due to the fact that	because
during the time that	while or when
factual data	data
first and foremost	first; most important
has made use of	uses
have a positive effect on	improve
I am of the opinion that	I think
I wish to inform you	*(omit)*
in order to	to
in reference to	about
in the event that	if
meet together	meet
on an individual basis	individually
plan in advance	plan
subsequent to	after
true facts	facts
we are not in the position to	we can't; we are unable to
we regret to inform you	unfortunately; we're sorry that
were in compliance with	complied with
with regard to	regarding; concerning; about

To remove deadwood, go through your writing and check every phrase for its relevancy. Either omit unnecessary words or replace them with simpler, more concise expressions. The above list is only a starting point. You will probably find other examples in your writing.

As you prune your writing, be sure you do not eliminate necessary as well as unnecessary information. In the process you may alter the material's meaning.

When writing is *too* spare, the reader often feels like the fish store owner who asked a sign painter to make a sign saying "Fresh fish sold here today." The sign painter pointed out that such a long message would cost a great deal. He suggested eliminating "today" since the fish were being sold now, not yesterday or tomorrow. The owner agreed. Then the sign painter pointed out that "here" was unnecessary as the fish would be sold only in the store. Again the owner agreed. "Sold" was not needed, the painter said, since no one expected the owner to give the fish away. And "fresh" was unnecessary because people did not expect stale or rotten fish. The owner sighed and agreed to a sign saying "Fish." But the painter had the last word. "Why do you need a sign saying 'Fish'? Everyone can smell them halfway down the street."

4. *Use parallel structure for coordinate ideas.* Expressions that are similar in content and function should be similar in form. The similarity in form makes it easier for readers to comprehend the similarity in concept. The Beatitudes are a classic example of parallel structure:

> Blessed are the poor in spirit: for theirs is the kingdom of heaven.
> Blessed are they that mourn: for they shall be comforted.
> Blessed are the meek: for they shall inherit the earth.

Would we remember the Beatitudes if they were written this way:

> Blessed are the poor in spirit: for theirs is the kingdom of heaven.
> They that mourn are also blessed, because they shall be comforted.
> And since the meek shall inherit the earth, they too are blessed.

More typical examples of nonparallel versus parallel structure are:

NONPARALLEL	PARALLEL
The sergeant must check the manuals regularly, and all new entries must be initialed by him.	The sergeant must check the manuals regularly and must initial all new entries. (*active voice in both parts of sentence*)
Employees may make the trip either in their personal cars or they can use state vehicles from the motor pool.	Employees may make the trip either in their personal cars or in state vehicles from the motor pool. (*parallel phrases following "either" and "or"*)

As you can see, parallel sentences sound better and are more concise.

Parallel structure is especially important when you are listing steps in a procedure. If one item in the list begins with an action verb, such as "File the yellow copy in the pending file," all items in the list should begin the same way.

5. *Avoid dangling and misplaced modifiers.* Place clauses and prepositional phrases next to the nouns they modify. Failure to do this can alter the sentence's meaning, sometimes to the point of ridiculousness. Here are some examples:

INCORRECT	CORRECT
After the physician's examination, the admissions clerk interviews the patient.	The admissions clerk interviews the patient after the physician examines him/her. (*The patient, not the clerk, is being examined.*)
Before being printed, the review committee must approve each new procedure.	The review committee must approve each new procedure before it is printed. (*The procedure, not the committee, is being printed.*)

This type of error is most likely to occur with long, involved sentences.

6. *Avoid misplaced and dangling participles.* As you probably remember from grade school, a participle is a verb form that functions as an adjective. Present participles end in *ing* (declining, endorsing, holding), while past participles end in *ed, t, en, n,* or *d* (estimated, bent, broken, known, told). Perfect participles combine "having" with the past participle of the main verb (having estimated, having broken, having known).

A participle is misplaced when it is too far from the noun or pronoun it is meant to modify and, as a result, appears to modify another word. Some examples of misplaced participles are:

MISPLACED	CORRECT
Hidden under the desk, I found the missing policy.	I found the missing policy hidden under the desk. (*The policy, not "I," was hidden.*)
Receiving a ten-year service pin, her supervisor congratulated her.	Her supervisor congratulated her for receiving a ten-year service pin. (*The employee, not the supervisor, received the pin.*)

A dangling participle occurs when the noun or pronoun the participle is meant to modify is not stated but only implied in the sentence. Here are two examples of dangling participles:

DANGLING	CORRECT
Being unhappy with the job, his work was unsatisfactory.	Being unhappy with the job, *he* did unsatisfactory work. (*subject clearly stated*)
Young and inexperienced, the job of procedures analyst seemed easy to me.	Young and inexperienced, *I* thought the job of procedures analyst would be easy. (*subject clearly stated*)

Participle problems are most likely to occur when you begin a sentence with a participle. To avoid problems, be sure the participial phrase is next to the word it modifies.

7. *Avoid buzz words and jargon.* Many business writers deliberately choose words and phrases for their "professional" sound. They also tend to replace simple one-syllable words like "use" with elaborate words like "utilize." The end result is organizational language that is unintelligible to outsiders as well as to many within the organization. A classic example is the U.S. Postal Service's definition of a mailbox:

> A manually operated automatic input device designed to discourage retrieval of input material by the operator.

Such writing defeats the purpose of a manual. Manuals are intended to be understood. Their objective is to get users to act in a particular way. If users cannot understand a manual, they certainly won't follow it. Here are some examples of buzz words and jargon. You can undoubtedly add others from your organization.

accountability
businesswise, profitwise, policywise, and so on
expedite
expertise
facilitate
impact (used as a verb: the new program *impacted* our profits favorably)
interface (when used to mean "meet with" or "work together") in a non-data processing application)
optimize, maximize, finalize, and so on
parameter (used incorrectly for "perimeter": a parameter is an arbitrary constant; a perimeter is the boundary or distance around an area)
profitability
specify methodology

8. *Be clear.* This rule sounds obvious, but think back: How many unintelligible or confusing policies and procedures have you read? Lack of clarity is a key problem in many manuals. Obviously, eliminating deadwood and jargon is one way to add clarity.

Here are two other tips for making your writing clear. First, if you have the slightest doubt whether a document is clear, have someone else read it and tell you in his or her own words what you meant. If your "test reader" has any difficulty with the document, rewrite it.

Having someone else review your writing for clarity is a good general policy. One procedures writer I know uses his ten-year-old son as a test reader; other writers use their secretary or a co-worker. The person you choose as a reader should not be an expert on the subject. Experts are often so familiar with a topic that they can mentally translate unclear material. But to the nonexpert user, the material is unclear.

Here's the second tip. Break up long, involved sentences into two or more shorter ones. Also check that every word you use is necessary and that every idea is expressed in the simplest possible language.

9. *Be human.* Remember that you are writing for people, not computers. One of the most dehumanizing instructions I've ever read was a procedure in the "emergency" section of a bank manual. If a customer in the bank had a heart attack, the teller was to call the head cashier, not an ambulance. Why I don't know—perhaps to close the account.

Less severe examples of such writings are found in personnel manuals or handbooks. Employees are lectured on their responsibilities with no mention made of their rights or the company's responsibilities to employees. Moreover, many sentences begin with "Employees shall not" or "must not" instead of stating positively what should be done. Manuals like these do much to demotivate employees.

THE GREAT HE/SHE CONTROVERSY

How do you handle the he/she problem in writing? People are sometimes offended if you just use "he," but what can you do instead? Unfortunately, there's no easy answer to this question. Since a manual should motivate readers, not offend, I recommend that you not automatically use "he" to refer to both sexes. Conversely, do not automatically use "she" to refer to secretaries and clerical personnel.

There are many ways to eliminate "he" and "his" from your writing. However, no one method works well in all situations. You have to choose the most appropriate style for each situation. Here are several options:

1. Reword the sentence to use plural pronouns. "They," "their," and "theirs" are blessedly neutral. So whenever possible, make a sentence plural.

Change: The employee should take advantage of *his* benefits.
    To: Employees should take advantage of *their* benefits.

2. Replace the pronoun with the noun it represents. This approach often works well for "he" but may become awkward with "his," as in the following example:

The operator should keep the operator's work station tidy.

3. Omit third-person pronouns altogether. You can sometimes do this by switching to the second person ("you") or by using a command verb with the "you" understood. And at times, "his" is unnecessary and can be omitted or replaced with "the." (For example, with a sentence like, "The machine operator should turn in his protective headgear at the end of his shift," substitute "The machine operator should turn in the protective headgear at the end of the shift.")

4. Use "he/she," "he or she," "his/her," or "his or her." The occasional use of these terms is acceptable, but they become awkward when used repeatedly.

5. Include a disclaimer stating that throughout the manual "he" stands for "he or she." The drawback to such a statement is that it may be overlooked, or may even draw attention to the issue.

6. Use "he" sometimes and "she" sometimes, often in alternate paragraphs. This practice is becoming fairly common in the academic world, but it is disconcerting and confusing to some readers.

7. Use "(s)he." There are two problems with this approach. First, "his" is still an unresolved dilemma. Second, since reading "s(he)" aloud is virtually impossible, readers tend to stumble over the word when they encounter it in print.

Since none of these options is totally satisfactory, you will probably find a combined strategy to be most effective. When possible, reword the sentence in the plural form. If that is not possible, either replace the pronoun with the noun it represents or omit the pronoun altogether. As a last resort, use "he or she" and "his or her." These forms are preferable to "he/she" and "his/her" simply because they sound better.

WRITING REFERENCES

Obviously, this section has covered only a few of the most common writing problems. If you will be doing much writing, you should invest in several reference works on the subject. The two listed below are "musts":

Strunk, William, and White, E. B., *The Elements of Style,* Macmillan (3rd ed., paperback, 1979). If you own only one book on writing, this should be it. It is inexpensive and highly readable.

A Manual of Style, University of Chicago Press. Adopt this book, or *Words into Type,* Prentice-Hall, or some other style manual as your bible for rules of punctuation, grammar, editing, and so on.

Here are a few more helpful references. In most cases, I've omitted publication dates and edition numbers because new editions (and less expensive paperback editions) are released frequently. Check with your bookstore to be sure you are getting the latest edition.

Bernstein, Theodore M., *The Careful Writer: A Guide to English Usage,* Atheneum Press.

Brusaw, Charles T., Alfred, Gerald J., and Oliou, Walter E., *The Business Writer's Handbook,* St. Martin's Press.

Fowler, H. W., *A Dictionary of Modern English Usage,* Oxford University Press.

Instant Spelling Dictionary, Career Institute. A spelling dictionary shows spellings and syllable divisions only; it does not define words. Consequently, it's very small and easy to refer to.

Roget, Peter M., *Roget's International Thesaurus,* Thomas Y. Crowell Co.

WRITING TECHNIQUES

In addition to following general principles of good writing, you should be aware of three writing techniques designed specifically for manuals.

Step-by-Step Listing

The first and most basic of these techniques is using step-by-step listing instead of long narrative paragraphs. In a manual, narrative paragraphs are often more difficult to follow than material presented in a listing format.

Although step-by-step listing is used primarily in procedures writing, it also works well for presenting complex multipart policies or any material that consists of a series of items. For example, if you wished to state the responsibilities of a particular position, you would list them rather than string them together in a long narrative paragraph.

Once you become accustomed to the step-by-step approach, you'll find it easier to write than conventional paragraphs—as well as easier for the user to read. To write a policy or procedure in step-by-step listing, follow these guidelines:

1. *Use a complete sentence ending in a colon to preface the items in the list.* Omit the introductory sentence if the title of the procedure serves the same function. There is no point in calling a procedure "Handling a Customer Complaint" and then beginning, "To handle a customer complaint, you should. . . ." However, you might begin a description of a position with "The responsibilities of the records manager are. . . ."

2. *List each step separately.* Listing items separately prevents confusion and ensures that the reader does not overlook an item.

3. *List the steps in an order that is logical to the reader.* For a procedure, list the actions in the order in which they should be performed. For a policy, list the items in descending order of importance, or perhaps group related items.

4. *Write each step as a complete sentence, preferably beginning with a command verb.* Partial sentences may confuse the reader. And command verbs like "use," "list," and "write" (with the subject "you" understood) make it clear that the reader is to perform the action.

5. *Use parallel structure throughout the list.* If you begin one item with a command verb, begin all the items that way.

6. *Use the active voice and the present tense.* As explained earlier, the active voice assigns responsibility, and the present tense makes it clear that the policy or procedure is in effect now. Complete the application for benefits as follows:

1. Fill in your Social Security number on line 1.
2. Review all information on the application and correct any errors.
3. Sign and date the application in the presence of a witness.
4. Have the witness sign the application.
5. Return the completed application to the personnel department.
6. Call the benefits administrator in the personnel department if you have any questions.

Playscript

Playscript, a writing technique developed by Leslie H. Matthies, is a further refinement of step-by-step listing. Playscript can be used most effectively with procedures that involve several different people or departments because it clearly defines each person's responsibilities. It can also be used for procedures involving only one person, but there is no particular advantage to doing so.

Playscript divides each step performed in the procedure into two parts: the actor (responsibility) and the action. The actor is named on the lefthand side of the page and the action is stated on the right. The actions are written in step-by-step listing. Here in playscript is a portion of a procedure for requesting office supplies:

Responsibility	Action
Secretary	1. Prepares supply requisition (Form 29-78).
Department manager	2. Approves and signs requisition.
Secretary	3. Files pink copy of Form 29-78 in pending file.
	4. Sends original and yellow copy of Form 29-78 to supply room.
Supply room clerk	5. Delivers all supplies requested to the secretary.
	5a. If some supplies are not available at this time, notifies secretary of approximate delivery date.

With playscripts there are three basic ways to handle exceptions. One way is by indenting and in not over five steps outlining the procedure for handling exceptions. This is the method used in 5a above. Another way is by indenting but referring the reader to another procedure. However, this type of cross-referencing is awkward and should be avoided if possible. The third way is to include (either as 5a or 6) a statement that exceptions to the procedure are to be referred to a particular person, such as the employee's supervisor. Of course, a job should be used here, not a person's name, just as is done in the responsibility column.

Because of its simplicity and versatility, playscript has become one of the most widely used writing techniques for manuals. It gives the reader a clear overview of a procedure and a precise description of his or her responsibilities. Keep in mind, however, that playscript should be used only for procedures. It does not adapt well to policy descriptions or other forms of writing.

Another potential problem with playscript is layout. Do not allow the responsibility column to occupy too much space. A good rule of thumb is to allow 2″ for the responsibility column, ¼″ between the responsibility and action columns, and 4″ for the action column. This system leaves ample margins and adequate space for the actions.

Although playscript is a valuable technique, it can descend to the ridiculous if it is used inappropriately. For example, in its procedure for handling robberies, one bank assigned specific responsibilities to a person titled "Robber." Among other things, Robber had to request the money by note. Apparently, if Robber asked for the money verbally, the teller would have to explain that this was not the correct procedure.

Action-Condition Logic

Up to now, we've discussed ways to describe a straightforward series of actions and responsibilities. The user performs step A, then B, then C, and so on. Or different individuals perform different steps, but the order in which they perform the steps remains constant. For these situations, step-by-step listing and playscript are ideal techniques. However, they are not adequate for complex if-then situations where a combination of conditions (or "ifs") must occur before the action ("then") is performed. For these situations, you should use action-condition logic.

As the name implies, action-condition logic reverses the traditional order of the if-then statement. The action is stated first, followed by the conditions or combination of conditions that must occur for that action to take place. The conditions are listed according to the guidelines for step-by-step listing. Both reversing the traditional order and listing the conditions clarify the material. The reader can easily determine when a particular action is to be performed.

To write a sentence in action-condition logic, follow these five guidelines:

1. *Find the verb for the action statement.* The verb tells what action is to be performed if all the conditions are met.

2. *Find the subject for the action statement.* The subject is usually the person who will perform the action if all the conditions are met.

3. *Write the action statement as an introductory sentence ending with "if:"* For example:

> "You may join the employee savings plan at the beginning of any pay period if:"

4. *Find the "and" and "or" conditions that must be met if the action is to be performed.* Remember that all conditions connected by "and" must be met if the action is to be performed, but only one of each set of "or" conditions must be met. For example, the following are "and" conditions:

> . . . you have been with the company at least one year, and you submit a completed enrollment form at least 30 days before the date you wish your membership to begin.

These are "or" conditions:

> . . . you are either a full-time employee or a part-time employee working at least 1,000 hours a year.

5. *List the conditions under the action statement, using step-by-step listing.* Show the user that the "or" conditions are subordinate to the "and" conditions and the "and" conditions are subordinate to the action statement. To indicate this subordination, indent and use an appropriate numeric or alphanumeric system.

Here's a complete example of action-condition logic:

You may join the employee savings plan at the beginning of any pay period if:

    a. you have been with the company at least one year, and
    b. you are either:
        (1) a full-time employee, or
        (2) a part-time employee working at least 1,000 hours a year, and
    c. you submit an enrollment form at least 30 days before the date you wish your membership to begin.

It's easy to determine from this statement exactly what must be done to enroll in the employee savings plan. Readers would find it more difficult to determine the requirements for enrollment if the material were written in a long narrative paragraph like this:

If you have been with the company at least one year either as a full-time employee or a part-time employee working at least 1,000 hours a year and if you submit an enrollment form at least 30 days before the date you wish your membership to begin, you may join the employee savings plan at the beginning of any pay period.

Now you have the tools for writing a manual—step-by-step listing, playscript, and action-condition logic. You've also reviewed the principles of effective writing. It is up to you to adapt these techniques to your manual and produce clear, concise copy that users can easily understand.

CHAPTER 8

Using Visual Support Techniques to Improve Communications

ALTHOUGH MOST MANUALS consist primarily of written text, certain visual aids can greatly enhance a manual and help the user better understand the material. The visual support techniques used most frequently in manuals are decision tables, flowcharts, and forms. This chapter discusses these three techniques as well as other types of useful illustrations.

DECISION TABLES

In Chapter 7 we examined action-condition logic as a way to express complex if-then situations in writing. Decision tables are another way to present the same if-then material. Often converting material to a table or chart makes it easier for the user to understand. Also, decision tables enable you to present a great deal of information in very compact format.

You can use decision tables either to replace a written text or to supplement and illustrate the text. In either case, the principle is the same: list the "if" conditions in separate columns and then list the actions that result from the "if" conditions. If more than one action results, each is listed in a separate column as well.

There are two types of decision tables: horizontal and vertical. As the names imply, horizontal decision tables are read from left to right and vertical decision tables are read from top to bottom. Here is a typical statement from a manual:

Nonexempt employees will receive overtime (time and a half) for work performed in excess of 40 hours weekly. Double time will be paid for all work performed on a Sunday or a company-designated holiday. Exempt employees will receive compensatory time off for all work performed in excess of 50 hours weekly.

Tables 1 and 2 show this statement in decision table form. Note that in the horizontal decision table (Table 1) the conditions are kept parallel. The first column lists the type of employee, and the second column states how many hours were worked. The third column gives the appropriate compensation (action) for each set of conditions. If an additional action were to be performed, it would be listed in a separate column under the heading *and then*.

The vertical decision table (Table 2) converts the conditions to questions that require a yes or no answer. For every logical combination of yes's and no's, the appropriate action is checked. Note that asking whether the employee is nonexempt is sufficient, because any employee who is exempt is clearly *not* nonexempt. Also, because of the nature of the material, some questions are not applicable.

The vertical decision table is primarily used by computer programmers and other data processing personnel, because it reduces each condition to a yes-no answer which the computer can "read." The chief drawback to the vertical table is that some material does

Table 1. Horizontal decision table: Compensation for work done outside of regular hours.

If	and if	then
Nonexempt employee	Works over 40 hours in week	Pay overtime at time and a half
Nonexempt employee	Works on a Sunday	Pay double time
Nonexempt employee	Works on a company holiday	Pay double time
Exempt employee	Works over 50 hours in week	Credit with compensatory time

not adapt well to a yes-no situation. Also, since people naturally read left to right, vertical listings can be confusing.

So unless you are writing a manual for EDP (electronic data processing) personnel, I recommend that you avoid vertical decision tables in your manuals. You may, however, find the vertical tables helpful for analyzing a policy or procedure and breaking it down into a series of small steps.

Horizontal decision tables are preferable to vertical tables in manuals. They are valuable for describing any situation that involves a variety of conditions and actions and are especially effective for outlining the options for employee benefit and pension plans and similar situations. Table 3 illustrates one company's life insurance benefits in decision table form.

Obviously, in addition to the table, the employee would be given a copy of the appropriate insurance policy. The value of the table is that it highlights the criteria for membership in the various plans and their respective benefits. Notice also that the table is written as concisely as possible, with all subjects and most verbs omitted.

Table 2. Vertical decision table: Compensation for work done outside of regular hours.

Condition				
Is employee nonexempt?	Yes	Yes	Yes	No
Did employee work over 40 hours in week?	Yes	N/A	N/A	Yes
Did employee work on Sunday?	No	Yes	No	N/A
Did employee work on company holiday?	No	No	Yes	N/A
Did employee work over 50 hours in week?	N/A	N/A	N/A	Yes
Action				
Pay overtime at time and a half	X			
Pay double time		X	X	
Credit with compensatory time				X

N/A = not applicable.

Table 3. Company-paid life insurance benefits.

If	*and if*	*then*	*and then*
Salary less than $15,000/yr.	Does not travel on company business more than once a quarter	Life insurance benefits 1½ times annual salary	No accidental death insurance
Salary less than $15,000/yr.	Travels on company business more than once a quarter	Life insurance benefits 1½ times annual salary	Accidental death insurance benefits of $50,000
Salary greater than $15,000/yr.	Does not travel on company business more than once a quarter	Life insurance benefits 2 times annual salary	No accidental death insurance
Salary greater than $15,000/yr.	Travels on company business more than once a quarter	Life insurance benefits 2 times annual salary	Accidental death insurance benefits of $100,000

FLOWCHARTS

You may be surprised to find flowcharts included in a discussion of visual support techniques for manuals. Many preparers of manuals assume that flowcharts belong only in data processing systems manuals. In fact, flowcharts can add a great deal to any type of procedure writing. You've already seen how effective PERT charts are in planning. And PERT charts are simply modified flowcharts.

When you strip away the data processing veneer, you'll find that a flowchart is just a "roadmap" for a procedure or system. Flowcharts are ideal for diagramming complex procedures that require a series of decisions, with a variety of actions resulting from each decision. Flowcharts can also serve as an overview or summary of a complicated work system. In that case, individual procedures are written for various portions of the system.

Flowcharts are not only valuable in the manual, but they're also a useful outlining technique. When writing a procedure, you may find it helpful to organize the steps in a flowchart before beginning to write.

When you include flowcharts in manuals for non-data processing personnel, use the fewest possible types of flowchart symbols. Otherwise, you may confuse or intimidate the readers. Try to limit the charts to the following three symbols:

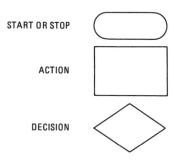

Practically all non-data processing flowcharts can be written with these three symbols. As a further aid to the non-data processing user, include an explanation of the symbols in a legend on the flowchart or in the manual's introduction. Plastic templates for drawing these and other flowchart symbols are available from most office supply stores.

Figure 8 is a flowchart for a billing and shipping procedure. It uses only the three flowchart symbols mentioned above, yet it is completely self-explanatory.

Figure 9 is a more humorous approach to flowcharting. When introducing flowcharts to non-data processing personnel, you may find it helpful to use an example. I've yet to find anyone who could not fully understand and appreciate this flowchart. After seeing Figure 9, on obtaining a soft drink, users find flowcharts much less intimidating.

So don't be afraid to use flowcharts in your manuals. Many organizations successfully use flowcharts in manuals designed for clerical personnel as well as those for management. The charts are an effective visual technique for all levels of employees.

One last word of advice: Because flowcharts condense a great deal of information, they should normally be used in conjunction

Figure 8. Flowchart for billing and shipping procedure.

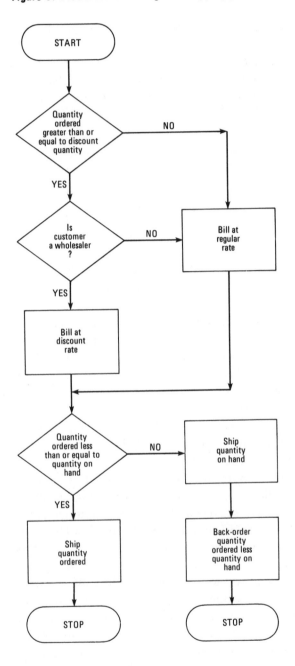

Figure 9. Flowchart for obtaining a soft drink.

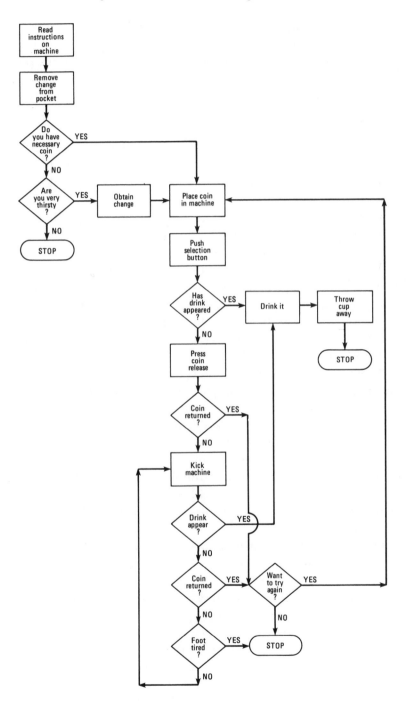

with a written text. The only time they should stand alone is when they are used to give an overview of an entire system—and even then, separate procedures should be written for the various portions of the system.

FORMS

Most manuals refer to various corporate and government forms and often include instructions on how to complete them. If these instructions and references are to be effective, they should follow certain guidelines.

1. All forms discussed in the manual should be reproduced in the manual. Thus users know exactly which form is being referred to and what the form looks like.

2. If you will be referring to the form in several places in the manual without explaining how to complete it, reproduce the form once in a special forms section at the back of the manual. Mention such a section in the "how to use this manual" portion of the introduction. Usually the forms in this special section are filed according to form number.

3. If you are explaining how to complete a form, reproduce the form on the page *facing* the instructions. Then the user can look at the form while reading the procedure without having to flip back and forth from the form to the directions.

4. Fill in the sample form facing the instructions, preferably using hand-printing. Then the user can see what the completed form looks like. If the sample completions are typed instead of printed, they tend to blend in with the instructions on the form. Also, a fine-line black felt-tipped pen will reproduce better than a ballpoint.

Of course, if you want users to type their answers rather than print them, you should say so in the procedure and show a form with the responses typed in. In this situation, use an italic typeface to complete the form so the user can easily differentiate the responses from the printed form.

5. Use code numbers or letters to link steps in the procedure with specific parts of the form. For example, if step 2 is to write the order number from the bill of lading on the appropriate blank of

the form, designate that blank with a 2 also. Figure 10 indicates this technique.

6. You may need to reduce the form slightly so it will fit on a page in the manual, but beware of overreduction. It's extremely discouraging to have to pore over a sample with a magnifying glass trying to decipher what it says.

7. Don't include actual copies of forms in the manual. Most forms are printed on very thin paper that is not durable enough for use in a manual. Also, most forms are not designed to be three-hole punched, and the holes frequently end up in the body of the form. Perhaps most important, if you include actual blank forms in the manual, the user may be tempted to remove the form and use it instead of getting one from the supply cabinet.

8. If the procedure for completing the form is more than one page long, reproduce the entire form on the first facing page. On subsequent pages, reproduce the segment of the form that is being discussed. For example, if the instructions for completing a particular section of a claims form are given on the third page of the procedure, reprint that section *only* on the page facing those instructions. This technique prevents unnecessary repetition, yet spares the reader from having to look back or remove the sample from the binder.

9. In the index to the manual, include all forms mentioned in the manual. List the forms alphabetically by title or subject under the general heading "Forms." If the forms are kept in the manual by form number in a special forms section, you do not need to list

Figure 10. Coding a form.

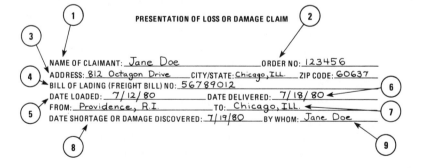

them by number in the index. However, if the forms are located throughout the manual, they should also be indexed by number.

10. If a multipurpose form is used for different procedures, discuss the various ways of completion as part of the various procedures, rather than all together. If you discuss them all at once, the user may become confused and have difficulty determining which method of completion is right for a particular situation. Of course, the various uses of the form should be clearly indicated in the index.

If directions for completing the form are an integral part of the various procedures, reproduce the form in each procedure. Otherwise, reproduce it once in the forms section of the manual.

OTHER ILLUSTRATIONS

Although decision tables, flowcharts, and forms are the visual aids used most frequently in manuals, you should not feel restricted to these types of artwork. Depending on the type of manual, you may also wish to include:

Diagrams, sketches, or photographs
Location charts or maps
Graphs
Organization charts
Copies of computer printouts
Cartoons or humorous drawings

1. Diagrams and sketches are cheaper to reproduce than photographs and do not become "dated" as quickly. Therefore, you should use sketches or line drawings instead of photographs, whenever possible. Sometimes, however, with complex equipment, photographs are necessary to show sufficient detail.

In particular, avoid using photographs of people. Changes in hair and clothing styles quickly make such photos look dated. Also, they can lead to embarrassing situations. One company I know used staff photographs in an employee handbook. Shortly afterward, one of the employees included in the book was involved in a local scandal and left the company abruptly. The photograph became an object of ridicule, and the page had to be reprinted.

Diagrams and sketches can really enhance a policy or procedure.

For example, a sketch showing how to read a measuring device such as a tachometer can be invaluable to the user.

2. Organization charts are appropriate for some policy and personnel manuals, but they should not include people's names. Depending on the turnover rate in your organization, such a chart can become out of date even as it is being printed. Lists of names belong in a corporate directory or similar publication that is easier to change and less expensive to produce. In fact, people's names should not appear anywhere in your manual. Instead, use job titles.

3. If you are going to show computer printouts in your manual, be sure that they reproduce well. In many cases, the reproduction is so faint as to be virtually unreadable. If your printer cannot make legible copies of the printout, you are better off preparing a typed mockup of the printout.

4. Beware of "clip art" clichés. Some commercial art firms offer booklets of line drawings that portray standard scenes of people at work or at leisure, holiday and seasonal themes, and so on. These booklets are relatively inexpensive, and the purchase of one entitles you to reproduce all the drawings in it. You simply cut out the drawings and paste them on the page—hence the name clip art.

Clip art is common in employee handbooks—all those sketches of smiling employees at work. The problem is that most clip art is trite and boring, and usually looks dated. There are some exceptions to this statement, but generally speaking you should avoid clip art as a means of illustration.

5. Cartoons or humorous sketches may be appropriate in some manuals, particularly employee handbooks and user guides to company services (the print shop, mail room, and so on). You can use such drawings to make a point tactfully or to make a manual more readable. For example, in a manual for users of the company's various administrative services, you might include a sketch of a perplexed print shop manager holding several requisitions boldly marked ASAP (as soon as possible). The manager is being confronted by a secretary who is holding a large stack of copy and saying, "Could we have 200 copies of this by 9:00 A.M. tomorrow?" Such a drawing can make its point more effectively than pages of directives telling employees that the print shop needs x days to print y copies of z pages.

Of course, humorous artwork is not appropriate in all manuals.

And some organizations are more receptive than others to a light approach. So proceed with caution here. If you're not sure whether a humorous touch is appropriate, it probably isn't.

CRITERIA FOR USING ILLUSTRATIONS

When deciding if you should include illustrations in a manual, ask yourself these questions:

1. Is the manual an appropriate place for this material? Or would it be better suited to an organization directory, employee newsletter, management report, or other communications tool?

2. Does the illustration make the manual easier to understand or use? For example, a sketch of a portion of a machine may improve the user's understanding of the procedure.

3. Is the illustration included to satisfy someone's ego rather than to increase understanding? A photograph of a key company officer is an excellent example of the "ego" illustration.

4. Will the illustration become dated or obsolete quickly? Examples of this type of illustration are photographs of people and organization charts with names.

If you can answer "yes" to the first two questions and "no" to the last two, you should definitely include the illustration in the manual. Remember, there are few fixed rules as to what illustrations are appropriate. In making your choice, you should be guided by good taste and common sense.

CHAPTER 9

The Review Process: Turning a Mountain into a Molehill

AFTER A MANUAL or a portion of a manual is written and illustrated, the next step is having the material reviewed. Traditionally, the review process is a major roadblock in the development of a manual. The preparer must coordinate the reviewers' efforts and ensure that the copy is promptly reviewed. Since the reviewers frequently outrank the manual preparer in the corporate hierarchy, coordinating the reviews may take tact and diplomacy. However, if you plan your review strategy carefully, you can avert or at least minimize most problems.

WHO SHOULD REVIEW THE MANUAL?

The first major consideration is determining who should review the manual. Review structures vary greatly from organization to organization. Some manuals are only reviewed by two individuals; others have as many as twenty reviewers. But instead of specifying an arbitrary number of reviewers, I recommend a review process which includes four different types of reviews.

First, someone knowledgeable in the subject area should review the copy for content and accuracy. This person does not necessarily have the authority to approve the manual for company use. However, he or she should be an expert on the subject and should be able to determine if the manual's contents are accurate. If a manual covers a number of different areas, you may need to have several people review the different portions. Or you may want to have more than one person review a particular section for content. The latter situation is especially common with policy manuals.

Second, a member of the organization's legal staff should also review the manual. If your company does not have a legal staff, whoever serves as legal counsel should conduct the review. The review ensures that the manual complies with all relevant legislation and meets the requirements of any regulatory bodies that have jurisdiction over your organization. A legal review is especially important for policy manuals, personnel manuals, accounting and finance manuals, and any manuals distributed outside the organization. The Equal Employment Opportunity Act, ERISA (Employee Retirement Income Security Act), OSHA (Occupational Health and Safety Act), and the Foreign Corrupt Practices Act are just a few of the laws that may affect the content of such manuals.

Failure to review carefully for legality could result in a major lawsuit. Of course, even with legal review, litigation could occur; however, the risk is substantially less. Also you, the manual preparer, have protected yourself by getting a legal opinion.

The third type of review is for quality of writing and clarity. The person who performs this review should be thoroughly familiar with the principles of effective writing. The reviewer may come from the department preparing the manual or from corporate communications.

Ideally, you should supplement the professional writing review with an evaluation by a potential user of the manual—someone relatively unfamiliar with the subject. If this person can understand the material and explain it correctly to you in his or her own words, you can be reasonably confident that the writing is clear and easy to understand.

The final review must, of course, be made by someone with the authority to approve the manual for company use. The other reviews can be scheduled simultaneously, but this review should take place after all the others. Also, all appropriate changes and corrections requested by the previous reviewers should be made before the final review.

Along with these reviews, you may need to schedule "courtesy" reviews by members of departments not directly affected by the manual. Asking them to review the material helps to prevent conflicts in policies and procedures. Such reviews should definitely be scheduled simultaneously.

Try to keep the total number of reviewers to a minimum. If ten or fifteen people must review the manual and reach agreement, the manual may become obsolete before it is printed—or it may never be printed. Such reviews are usually designed to assuage egos and make people feel important rather than to ensure accuracy.

However, there should be more than one or two reviewers. It's easy for one or two people to overlook an error. Also, one or two people are not likely to be able to perform all four types of reviews.

THE REVIEWER'S RESPONSIBILITIES

One way to reduce reviewing problems is to meet with your reviewers ahead of time and discuss their role in the manual's preparation. At the meeting, stress both the reviewers' responsibilities and your desire to assist the reviewers in every way. If possible, meet with all reviewers at once to save time and to make the reviewers feel comfortable. If this is impossible, meet with each one separately to discuss the review process and his or her role in it.

Most reviewers are not fully aware of their responsibilities. They feel that their only duties are to approve and return the material. Actually the reviewer's responsibilities are much more extensive and include the following:

1. *To review the material fairly and objectively.* Reviewers should evaluate the manual on its own merits. Some reviewers allow office policies or their personal feelings or prejudices to intrude on their judgment. This is a difficult situation to resolve, but making reviewers aware of the problem can do much to reduce it.

2. *To concentrate on the topic or area they have been requested to review.* For example, the lawyer should concentrate on the manual's legality rather than on its grammar and style. If the reviewers spot an obvious problem unrelated to their area, they should point it out. However, they need not look actively for problems in other areas. Most reviewers greatly appreciate being responsible only for those areas they are knowledgeable in.

3. *To provide specific, constructive criticism.* Comments such as "That's poorly written" and "I don't understand this" give the writer no guidelines for improvement and are usually demoraliz-

ing. Constructive comments like "the sentences in this paragraph are too long," "I don't think that the user will know what this means," and "I don't understand what you do if the employee applies for a transfer" give the writer specific problems to solve.

4. *To be positive in their criticism, stating what was done well as well as what areas need improvement.* The manual writer is not unique in needing an occasional pat on the back. The reviewer's job is to commend as well as to criticize. Unfortunately, many reviewers neglect this aspect of reviewing. They mistakenly feel they have discharged their duty by correcting any errors.

5. *To review carefully the first time and make all major changes then.* Many reviewers make an initial cursory review, reasoning that they will see the manual again later in the review process, and can make other suggestions then. This type of thinking destroys scheduling and practically guarantees production delays. Explain to your reviewers that all major changes should be made at the first review and that any subsequent reviews are for fine-tuning the revised copy.

6. *To avoid requesting changes that can be explained only on the grounds of personal taste.* We all express ourselves in different ways. Reviewers should not expect the preparer of the manual to write as they do. They should require that the writing be clear and concise, but they should also allow the writer some flexibility in diction and style.

7. *To review promptly and to return the material by the agreed-upon deadline.* This last responsibility undoubtedly gives the preparer of the manual more headaches than any other part of the review process. For a variety of reasons, many reviewers appear incapable of meeting a review deadline.

ENSURING THAT REVIEWERS MEET DEADLINES

A multifaceted strategy works best in overcoming the recurrent reviewer deadline problem. Here are the steps to follow:

1. *Publicize top management support for the manual.* A short letter or memo signed by the organization's president or an appropriate vice president does wonders. The memo states that you or your staff is in charge of preparing the manual and asks everyone to give you

his or her full cooperation. The memo serves as your advance billing. It lets everyone know that the manual is an important project that has full support from top management. To ensure that the memo goes out, you may want to draft it yourself and submit it to the executive, who will approve and sign it.

2. *Negotiate review schedules instead of setting arbitrary deadlines.* When people set their own deadlines, they are much more likely to meet them. Explain to the reviewer what is to be reviewed and when it will be ready for review. Then ask the reviewer how long it will take to go over the material.

If the reviewer's time estimate is less than or equal to the amount of time you'd like to allow, tell the reviewer, "That's great; thank you!" If the estimate is longer than you'd like, begin making distress noises—something to the effect that you won't be able to get the copy to the printer in time for distribution by the date you promised the president. Or make whatever remarks are necessary to indicate the urgency of the situation. Offer to help the reviewer in any way you can to speed up the process. Usually you will be able to negotiate a compromise. If not, discuss the situation with your boss or the reviewer's boss, or both.

Allowing the reviewer to set his or her deadline has another advantage. Reviewers in the upper levels of the organization sometimes resent being given a deadline by someone from a lower organizational rank. For example, I once encountered a rather chauvinistic vice president who resented getting a deadline from me. In the time he spent bombarding the other vice presidents with memos about my effrontery, he could have reviewed the manual six times. I soon realized this was an ego problem that could easily be avoided by letting the reviewer set the deadline. I changed techniques and had no further problems with this person.

Obviously, it would be tedious and time-consuming to negotiate a new review schedule every time you prepare an update. Instead, negotiate the schedule for review up-dates once and have the reviewer notify you if he or she cannot meet the agreed-upon deadline for a particular item.

3. *Confirm the agreed-upon deadline in writing.* If necessary, send copies to any appropriate individuals, such as the reviewer's boss. A written confirmation is an essential follow-up to the verbal negotia-

tions. The confirmation ensures that reviewers do not forget what they promised. Whether you carbon anyone in or not depends on whether doing so will motivate or irritate the reviewer. In most cases you're better off either not carboning anyone in or using "blind" carbons.

4. *Give reviewers a "friendly reminder" a few days before the deadline.* A friendly reminder to reviewers is not a dunning notice from a collection agency, but it has the same general effect. The friendly reminder is a phone call from you or a member of your staff ostensibly asking if the reviewer has any questions you could help with. In reality, it politely reminds the reviewer that the deadline is approaching.

If you can't reach reviewers directly to deliver the friendly reminder, work through their secretaries. With top management the secretary can often be more effective than you in getting a response.

5. *You may want to state in your confirming memo that if the material is not returned by the deadline, you will consider it approved.* Using this approach is somewhat like handling a live hand grenade. It can be very successful in overcoming the opposition or it can be fatal to you.

If you do decide to adopt this approach, couple it with a friendly reminder. One preparer of manuals I know sent out a policy for review using this method. The policy was not returned by the deadline, so the preparer had it printed as is—with a major error. The reviewer had been out of town for the entire review period and had never seen the policy. So if you adopt this approach, be sure the reviewer has in fact received the material.

This approach works well for the "courtesy reviews" discussed earlier—reviews where a number of people check to see that the manual does not conflict with their departmental practices. However, do not use it for the final review by the person who is to authorize publication. Here you should have a written approval to protect both you and the company.

Usually these five techniques in combination solve the problem of the recalcitrant reviewer. If they do not, review the situation with your boss to determine if a more authoritarian approach should be used.

OTHER REVIEWING TIPS

Here are a few other pointers for simplifying the review process and eliminating problems.

1. *If possible, give the manual to the reviewers in small, manageable portions rather than all at once.* Giving reviewers a section at a time is more efficient. The reviewers are not overwhelmed and demoralized by having to approve two hundred or more pages at once. And with a small section, they review more carefully. This helps reduce corrections later on. The sectional approach is easier for you also. As each section is approved, you can prepare it for production and even send it to the printer. The whole process is more efficient.

2. *If possible, limit review periods to two weeks or less.* When you allow over two weeks, reviewers tend to postpone the task or, worse yet, forget that they have material to review. The actual act of reviewing is not that time-consuming; the difficulty is getting the reviewer to set aside time for the task. And a relatively short deadline is a motivator. The two-week time period is usually more than sufficient if the reviewer is approving the manual in small sections.

3. *Attach a review form to the material being reviewed.* This form includes (1) the agreed-upon deadline, (2) the area being reviewed (content, legality, and so on), (3) instructions for reviewing (such as marking changes on the copy), and (4) a request that the reviewer sign the form to indicate that the copy is approved with changes as marked or with no changes. Such a form ensures that the reviewer is aware of all necessary information when the review takes place.

4. *Have the reviewer initial each page of the reviewed copy as well as sign the cover form.* Initialing each page serves two purposes:

(a) It motivates the reviewer to read each page. Some unenergetic reviewers are tempted to skim the material and then sign the cover form. Having to initial each page makes them more conscientious.

(b) Initialing protects you in case of controversy. If a problem arises later, an unscrupulous reviewer might claim that he or she never saw the material. Initialing indicates that the page was read and forces the reviewer to accept responsibility.

5. *Give the reviewer typed copy as it would appear in the manual.* You

may double-space the copy for ease in editing, but don't try to save time by giving the reviewer a rough draft filled with "typos" and penciled-in corrections. Such copy is difficult to read and irritating. It's like serving someone a formal dinner on a paper plate.

Also, when a reviewer sees marked, messy copy, he or she has trouble visualizing the finished product and begins making more changes. If the copy looks ready for the printer, the reviewer will be less tempted to make unnecessary changes.

6. *Whenever possible, schedule reviews simultaneously.* Some companies have one reviewer work on the material and then forward it to the next reviewer. This practice can take months. Also, one reviewer's delay will disrupt the whole process.

Simultaneous reviews controlled by you are more efficient. You send out the copies, and they are returned directly to you. You then compile the corrections. Conflicts can usually be resolved over the phone or through a quick meeting. Keeping tight control over the review process eliminates most problems.

CHAPTER 10

Steering Your Manual Through Production

AFTER THE MANUAL is reviewed and approved, your next task is to have copies prepared. Although the production process is mechanical rather than creative, it requires considerable coordination, and if it is not properly planned, it can cause substantial delays.

The first production step—the typing of drafts—has been going on during the writing and reviewing stages. But now it assumes primary importance, since most manuals are reproduced from typed copy rather than typeset. Consequently, this copy must be perfect.

WORD PROCESSING AND MANUALS PREPARATION

A steadily increasing number of companies are using word processing equipment for manuals preparation and other communications. Word processing commonly refers to any system of "automatic" or computerized typing equipment that records copy on a magnetic medium such as mag cards, tapes, or diskettes. The operator can make corrections or changes on the magnetic medium and print a new, correct copy without retyping the whole page or document. Obviously, this capability for making corrections and revisions is of great value in the production of manuals. Even extensive revisions can be made easily and accurately.

Because the technology of word processing is changing so rapidly, it is difficult to discuss it in detail in a book of this sort. You should, however, be aware of some special features of word processing that aid in the production of manuals. In future years, these features will undoubtedly be improved further.

The most important of these special features is the indexing capability, discussed in Chapter 6. If you are considering purchasing word processing equipment, the indexing feature is well worth the additional cost. Several manufacturers make systems with the capability to index.

Several word processing systems now have a "dictionary" feature that proofreads the text against the dictionary and corrects any misspelled words. This is a help, though hardly critical to your manual's success. And the more sophisticated systems allow you to add other words to the standard "dictionary."

Optical character recognition (OCR) is a great aid in the revision of manuals not now on magnetic media. The OCR reader scans the copy and automatically transcribes it on the magnetic medium. The operator need only key in changes rather than retype the whole manual. With OCR, typed drafts from other departments can be placed on tape or diskette and then edited without retyping. At this time, OCR readers can only read certain typefaces, but as the technology continues to improve, the number of scannable typefaces will increase.

With voice recognition equipment, now in its primitive stages, dictation is directly converted into typed copy with no need to key in the material. At this time, the equipment is very costly and does not always detect changes in voice patterns or accents accurately. Voice recognition is not practical now, but it was not long ago that the same statement could be made about word processing.

Another recent technological development that you should be aware of is the on-line or "paperless" manual. Here the printed (hard-copy) manual is totally eliminated. Instead, the text is entered into a computer and stored. Users "call up" the relevant portions of the manual on a computer terminal screen.

Obviously, this approach is cost-effective only when a large computer system and adequate terminals already exist in the company. And thorough indexing and cross-referencing are essential if material is to be found easily. Some large organizations have begun experimenting in this area, and a number of others are considering the on-line approach.

While on-line manuals have some definite advantages in terms of cost savings, ease of updating, and reduction of paperwork, there are also drawbacks. Browsing through an on-line manual is hardly feasible. Also, you will undoubtedly encounter some user resistance to the idea. And the manual is no longer portable.

A slightly less dramatic innovation is putting manuals on microfilm or microfiche. Again this is cost-effective only if the organization has microfilm or microfiche readers located near all users. If the readers are present, microfilming the manual is an economical approach. If a hard copy of a portion of the manual is needed, one can be made easily, though not cheaply, with a reader-printer. This approach is especially viable for banks and insurance companies, which usually have extensive micrographics equipment.

Despite these advantages, there are some definite drawbacks to microfilming manuals. Most microforms are difficult to update. Also, reading material on a microfilm or microfiche reader is much harder on the eyes than reading printed copy. As a result, users may make an excessive number of hard copies on the reader-printer. Finally, using microfilm and microfiche discourages browsing through the manual. Consequently, microfilm and microfiche are best used for reference manuals.

WORKING WITH YOUR WORD PROCESSING CENTER OR TYPISTS

Now that we've examined some of the more innovative approaches to producing manuals, let's take a brief look at the day-to-day reality of working with your word processing center. Word processing is still a very new and very young area. Consequently, many centers are going through growth pains. Be patient. It usually takes two to three years before a center reaches peak efficiency. Even then, the addition of or conversion to new equipment can cause upheavals.

You should get to know your word processing center personnel and their equipment. You may know the center manager by name, but have you ever asked for a tour of the center and information on its capabilities? If you haven't, do so. You'll gain a better understanding of the center and what it can do for you. Also, the simple act of showing interest often results in improved service.

The following guidelines will help you work more efficiently with your organization's typing or word processing personnel.

1. *Review the manual's format and layout with the typist or word processing operator.* As part of this review, it's a good idea to give the operator a sample page or two to demonstrate how you want the copy typed.

2. *If possible, work with only one or two operators or typists, instead of a whole center.* Then the operators will become familiar with the manual's special requirements, and you will not have to continually train new personnel. If you use two operators, you will have a backup if one gets sick or goes on vacation.

3. *Learn to dictate, especially if you have word processing.* Dictating is approximately four times faster for you than writing in longhand. And it's easier and faster for the operator to transcribe your dictation than to decipher your handwriting.

Dictating for manuals is obviously somewhat more difficult than dictating correspondence or reports. However, when you begin writing a policy or procedure, you probably develop a very rough draft or outline which only you can read. Of course, you can rewrite the material neatly and legibly for the typist or word processing operator. However, the process is very time-consuming. It's much faster to dictate from your notes or outline. Then the operator prepares a rough draft of the material. You edit the rough draft for spelling, punctuation, and content and return it to the operator so the corrections and changes can be made. With a well-managed center, this process is extremely efficient, saving both your time and the operator's.

If you feel nervous or self-conscious about dictating, build up your confidence by dictating short letters or memos. For example, dictation is an excellent way to handle those memos confirming time and price estimates for various portions of the manual.

Many word processing centers have guidelines and dictation training programs for center users. And some manufacturers of dictation equipment supply training materials. So plunge in! Dictating can be one of your biggest timesavers.

4. *Proofread your own work.* Even if the word processing operators or typists proofread their products (and most do), you should still double-check their work. They may not catch all the errors.

5. *For major projects, such as manuals, confirm in writing all time commitments made by the center.* This action protects you and encourages the center personnel to give accurate estimates.

6. *Give the word processing center your full cooperation by submitting copy and changes promptly.* Try not to make all your efforts "rush jobs." And follow the rules and procedures established by the center for its users.

Although you should cooperate with the center whenever possible, you should be in control. The people at the center are there to help you, not to specify how the manual should be laid out. If word processing personnel want to dictate page layout or other aspects of production, be firm. The manual should be prepared according to your specifications, not the word processing center's.

PRINTING THE MANUAL

After the final version of the manual is typed and approved, you are ready to go to press. You will have to make three major decisions about printing the manual.

Your first decision is whether to print the manual in house or to use an outside printer. Of course, you may have no choice. It may be company policy to print manuals in-house. Or your organization may not have a print shop, in which case you must go outside.

If you have a choice, remember this general guideline. In-house printing is usually slower, poorer in quality, and cheaper. However, the advantage of economy usually outweighs the disadvantages of slowness and lower quality. Of course, some in-house print shops have the equipment and staff to produce excellent work quickly, but most in-house shops are underfunded, overworked, and at times poorly managed.

If you decide to go outside with your manual, get bids from several printers. Unless your manual is a large run (several thousand copies), you are better off dealing with a small printer who has less elaborate equipment. Many large printing firms either will not accept a small order or cannot produce it economically. Also, your order is likely to get more attention from a small printer.

Be sure to visit the printers you are considering. See if their shops are clean and well organized. If a printing shop is dirty or messy, the printer is likely to show a similar lack of concern for your manual. Every good printer I have ever worked with had a clean, orderly shop.

Ask to see samples of the printer's work. And if your company has not used the printer before, obtain a list of clients and check a few references. Since most printers will show you only their best work and give names of satisfied customers, this approach does not guarantee a high-quality printer. However, if the samples are less than excellent or the references less than glowing, you should immediately reject the printer.

If all other points of comparison are equal, go with the printer who supplies the lowest bid. Just be sure the bids are for the same item—that is, the same quality of paper, the same number of copies, the same amount of collation, and so on. Otherwise, you'll be comparing apples and oranges.

After you have selected a printer, you must decide whether to have the manual typeset or reproduced from typed copy. You should consider having the copy typeset under any of the following conditions:

The manual is going to be distributed outside the organization.
The organization has in-house typesetting equipment.
The manual will be printed as a small booklet.

Otherwise, it is generally best to reproduce the manual from typed copy. Most manuals are prepared this way. With today's high-quality typewriters and word processing equipment, the overall appearance of these manuals is quite satisfactory, and the cost savings are substantial.

Your third decision—choosing the method of printing—should be made with the aid of your outside printer or in-house print shop. The factors that affect your choice are:

The number of copies to be printed.
The types of equipment available.
The presence of any special artwork, such as photographs.

For very small runs (20 copies or less), you may find it most economical to photocopy the manual—provided your organization has a plain-paper photocopier that produces good copies. The exact cut-off point depends on whether you own or lease your copier, the type of copier you have, and the other types of equipment available.

For larger runs, your chief options are usually paper-plate offset or photo-offset with metal plates. In either case, the copy is transferred to a plate (paper or metal) and then reproduced. Paper plates are good for up to 1,500 copies but cannot be used effectively for photographs or very elaborate artwork. Metal plates are used for photographs and larger runs. The metal plates can be saved so more copies can be printed at a later date, but the paper plates cannot. Finally, the metal plates produce work of superior quality, but the difference is not so great as to justify the additional expense.

When choosing the method of printing, consult with your printer to determine which technique best meets your specifications and which is most cost effective. It's also a good idea to inspect samples printed by each method so you can compare quality. In most cases, you'll find the quality differences are relatively minor. If so, you should select the least expensive method.

TIPS ON PRINTING

Here are a few guidelines to aid you in working with your printer.

1. Prepare a "dummy" of your manual. A dummy is a mockup of the manual showing what appears on both sides of every page, which pages are left blank, where the tabs are positioned, and so on. To prepare a dummy, make a photocopy of the original typed or typeset copy and assemble it exactly as you wish the final product to be printed.

It's easier for the print shop staff to work from a dummy than from a list of instructions on an order or a requisition form. And a dummy substantially increases your chances of having the manual printed without upside-down pages or improperly placed tabs. The dummy is especially important if the manual is printed in-house. Printing a manual is a major project for most in-house shops, and you should provide them with as much help as possible.

2. *Use a nonphoto blue pencil to write any special printing instructions on the master copy.* Nonphoto blue is visible to the eye but does not reproduce on printed copies. The pencils are available at any office supply store and are very useful for indicating to the printer how to position artwork and other instructions. You can also use the pen-

cils to write reminders to yourself and to indicate corrections to your typist.

3. *Tell the printer in advance how many tabs the manual will have.* The need to collate tabs by hand adds considerable time and expense to the assembly process. Notifying the printer in advance helps ensure an accurate estimate of costs and allows the printer to schedule appropriate personnel for collating.

4. *If you have never toured your print shop, do so.* You'll gain a better understanding of the shop's equipment and capabilities, and you'll establish a better rapport with the members of the printing department.

If you're having the manual printed in-house and you're satisfied with the print shop's work, send a memo expressing your appreciation to the print shop manager's boss and carbon in the manager. Everyone can use a word of praise, and the odds are you'll get even better service in the future.

PHYSICAL DISTRIBUTION

In Chapter 11, we'll discuss who should get copies of the manual and why. This section, however, covers the physical distribution of the manual.

If the mailroom hand-delivers the manuals or if you issue them to users at training sessions, physical distribution is not usually a problem. However, if you are shipping or mailing the manuals to your users, you should follow these guidelines to make sure your manuals arrive in good condition.

1. *Ship the manuals in heavy-duty corrugated cartons.* Your binder sales representative can usually supply cartons designed to hold one copy securely. These cartons are well worth the additional expense. If the manual is not well protected, it is likely to be damaged in transit.

If you're shipping a number of manuals to one location in one box, be sure the carton is strong enough to hold the binders and their contents safely. The cartons in which the empty binders were shipped from the manufacturer are usually not strong enough to hold the binders with their contents. Weigh one binder with its contents and multiply the weight by the number of manuals you plan to ship to a particular location. Then you'll know how strong a carton you'll need.

2. *Do not insert the contents in the binder before shipping.* Inserting the contents can damage both the paper and the binder rings. Instead, have the contents shrink-wrapped or held together with a paper band. Upon receipt, the user inserts the contents in the binder.

3. *If you will be shipping a large number of manuals, alert your mailroom manager in advance.* Then the manager can make any necessary arrangements to accommodate you. And be sure to ask how quickly the manuals will be shipped out.

STORAGE

Storing manuals is usually a problem, for two reasons. First, in large quantities, manuals are heavy and bulky. Second, you are faced with the problem of either keeping the stored manuals up to date or updating them as you release them. Both alternatives are awkward and time-consuming.

Although these problems cannot be solved completely, the following approach will reduce the difficulties. Keep two to six extra copies of the manual on hand and up to date to ensure that you have copies available for immediate distribution. The exact number you keep ready to go will depend on the frequency with which you issue the manuals.

As you issue copies, have additional ones printed or photocopied from an updated master copy. This procedure is relatively simple and ensures that users receive up-to-date copies. If your manual is on word processing equipment, it may be more practical to print the new copies directly from the updated tapes or diskettes.

If you cannot print copies as needed from a master copy, you should store the extra manual pages uncollated. Then when a policy or procedure is revised, you can simply discard the old pages and replace them with the new ones. With this method, additional copies are collated as needed, but again it is advisable to keep two to six copies updated and ready to issue.

If your additional copies must be collated by hand, look for low-cost labor. One university I know has students who work part time collating manuals. Another organization uses senior citizens who work part time. And a third organization sends the materials to be collated to a shelter workshop. All three alternatives provide work to people who need it while holding costs to a minimum.

Extra binders and tabs will have to be stored somewhere and brought out of storage as needed. It is much more cost-effective to store extra binders and tabs than to reorder in small quantities. As a rule of thumb, you should order sufficient binders and tabs for the new copies you expect to issue in the next five years.

CHAPTER 11

Keeping *Your* Manual in *Your* Organization

DISTRIBUTION, control, and security are important parts of any manuals program. Frequently organizations forget that (1) manuals are very costly to produce; (2) manuals belong to the organization, not to the individuals who are using them; and (3) manuals are practical working tools, not status symbols or bureaucratic burdens. As a result of these misconceptions, many organizations have problems with distribution, control, and security. This chapter will examine all three areas and offer practical suggestions for avoiding the most common pitfalls.

ASSIGNING MANUALS TO JOBS, NOT PEOPLE

Your first step in combatting the problems of distribution and control is to assign your manual to jobs, not people. For example, Arnold Adder should have an accounting department procedures manual, not because he is Arnold Adder but because he needs one to successfully perform his job as accounts payable supervisor. The nature of the job determines whether someone receives a manual.

Manuals are too expensive and valuable to distribute unnecessarily. If Inez Interviewer, director of personnel, wants a copy of the accounting department procedures manual but has no need for it, she would not receive one. The exception to this rule is that the president and possibly the vice presidents should have a complete set of manuals.

Let's carry the concept of assigning manuals to jobs one step further. Some employees do not need their own copy of a particular manual. Instead they should have access to a departmental copy. As a rule of thumb, if someone refers to a manual every day or several times a week, that person should have a personal copy. If the employee refers to the manual less frequently, he or she need only have access to a departmental or work group copy.

Departmental copies are effective only if certain guidelines are followed. First, one person and one person only should have the responsibility for updating the manual. If updating is delegated to a group or department, it will never be done. Often the departmental secretary or administrative assistant is a logical choice for keeping the manual up to date. All revisions and updates are sent directly to this person.

If the group is a large one—over ten people—you may find it advisable to assign more than one copy of the manual to the group. The frequency of use will determine if extra copies are needed.

Departmental manuals should be available to all members of the group at all times. Sometimes a supervisor or manager has responsibility for the department's copy of the manual and, instead of sharing it with the group, keeps it stored in his or her office. This action defeats the purpose of the departmental manual. It should be kept in a readily accessible bookcase or reference area so all employees who need it can use it. To avoid problems, you may need to assign a separate copy to the supervisor.

Properly used, departmental manuals can result in substantial cost savings through reduced distribution. The idea is also popular with employees, because they do not have to spend valuable time updating manuals they rarely look at.

You may also need to establish a procedure for handling requests for copies of the manual. While the system need not be elaborate, the employee should be required to justify the need for a copy before one is issued. You should also decide, based on frequency of use, whether an individual or a departmental copy is more appropriate.

These guidelines for distribution will ensure that the right people in the organization have access to the manual. Your next task is to maintain control of the manuals within the system.

MAINTAINING CONTROL

Assign a number to each copy of the manual, and keep a record of who has that copy. For example, you might assign Arnold Adder accounting department procedures manual #29. This technique helps prevent manuals from being misplaced or floating through the organization. Arnold knows he is accountable for the existence and well-being of manual #29.

Affixing the manual number and user's name to the manual is a relatively easy matter. You can attach self-adhesive labels to the manual's spine or inside front cover. The inside cover is preferable because the label is less likely to get dirty or get torn off by accident.

A more prestigious and more expensive approach is to have the binder manufacturer attach small, clear vinyl pockets to the inside front cover. You then insert an identification card in the pocket showing the manual's number and the name of the person to whom it is assigned. The card should also state that the manual is company property and can be reclaimed at any time. This statement is not mere puffery. When an employee leaves the company or changes positions, the manual should remain behind.

There are two important reasons for retaining the manuals. The first reason is security. You do not want your manuals to go to a competitor. And many of the people leaving your company will be joining a similar firm. Of course, security is not always a concern. Sometimes, as in the case of public utilities, government agencies, and state universities, the Freedom of Information Act requires that manuals be made available to the public. Even so, to minimize costs, these organizations should retrieve their manuals from departing employees.

This brings us to the second reason for retrieval: manuals are very expensive to produce. It is foolish to let a book that probably cost $30 to $100 a copy leave the organization. If you do let manuals leave, you will have to issue new copies to incoming employees. You could easily and unnecessarily spend several thousand dollars a year replacing manuals. Ideally the personnel or human resources department should be responsible for retrieving manuals from departing employees. Personnel should have a list of the manuals assigned to each job position and, as part of the exit interview, should retrieve those manuals and return them to the department(s) issuing them.

If your personnel staff is not now doing this, ask them to incorporate the retrieval of manuals into the exit interview process. Your responsibility is to keep personnel supplied with an accurate list of who has which manual. If there is no exit interview procedure, either your department will have to retrieve the manuals or you will have to delegate responsibility to the employee's supervisor. Quite frankly, these methods are stopgap measures. Your organization should be conducting exit interviews to determine why employees leave, to inform employees about benefits that may be carried over, and so on. The retrieval of manuals is just one more reason for an exit interview. One organization I know holds the employee's final paycheck until all company property (including manuals) is returned—a most effective technique.

Of course, retrieval is not necessary for departmental manuals. If the manual's updater leaves, the department manager simply delegates the responsibility to another employee. And if the manual is not confidential and is printed in a small throwaway booklet, retrieval is also unnecessary.

Do not immediately reissue the manual to the employee now assuming the position. The new employee's predecessor may not have kept the manual up to date, and you will be handicapping the new employee by giving that person an incomplete or partially obsolete manual. Someone in your department should check the manual and update it as needed before reissuing it. At this time, the identifying label or card on the inside front cover should also be changed.

COPYRIGHTING—A SIMPLE BUT OFTEN NEGLECTED PROCEDURE

Manuals can and often should be copyrighted, particularly if you are concerned about protecting proprietary information. If you do not copyright, you have no legal protection against plagiarism. If your organization is a public agency or if it is in a noncompetitive field, you may not need protection. However, as a general rule, businesses should copyright their manuals.

Copyrighting is not the complex process most people think it is.

To copyright any material in the United States, write to the Register of Copyrights, Library of Congress, Washington, D.C., requesting current information on copyrighting and copyright application forms. These items will be sent to you free of charge.

When the manual is printed, include a copyright statement on the back of the title page. This statement constitutes the act of copyrighting and looks like this:

© 1980 by Acme Widgets, Inc.
All rights reserved.
Printed in the United States of America.

For additional legal protection, it is advisable to register the copyright. As soon as the manual is printed, send two copies of it, a completed copyright application form, and a check for $10.00 to the Register of Copyrights. In six to eight weeks, you will receive an official notice that the manual has been registered with the copyright office.

You need not recopyright the manual every time it is updated. Instead, recopyright for major revisions only. Since manuals usually have a steady stream of minor updates which have the cumulative effect of a major revision, I generally recommend recopyrighting every three to five years.

Canadian copyright procedures are somewhat simpler. You do not have to register your manual to obtain a copyright. Instead, print the manual with the following statement on the back of the title page:

© Acme Widgets, Ltd. 1980

The mere act of printing the manual with that statement copyrights the publication in Canada.

You may also, if you wish, register the manual with the Copyright and Industrial Design Branch, Bureau of Intellectual Property, Department of Consumer and Corporate Affairs, Ottawa. However, such registration is not necessary for legal protection. The registration fee is $25.00 (Canadian).

Obviously, none of the security controls is foolproof. People do reproduce copyrighted material illegally. And if someone is determined to take a copy of your manual to a competitor, he or she will find a way—usually by photocopying all or portions of the manual. However, most people will be deterred by the techniques outlined in this chapter (control numbers, retrieving copies, and copyrighting). And whether or not you are concerned about security, you should retrieve manuals from departing employees as a cost-control measure.

CHAPTER 12

Motivating the Manual's Users

YOUR ROLE in preparing the manual does not end when the manual is printed and distributed to its users. The development of a manual is an ongoing process, and a major part of that process is motivating recipients of the manual to use it. Unless they use the manual, the time and money spent producing it have been wasted.

Of course, a well-designed, well-written manual is much more likely to be used than an unattractive and unintelligible manual. But a well-prepared manual is not sufficient by itself. Most employees are so inundated by paperwork and superfluous corporate documents that, quite understandably, they are very resistant to any new corporate publications. Your goal is to overcome this resistance.

INTRODUCING THE MANUAL TO ITS USERS

Few things are more demoralizing than having the company mail carrier drop a 200-page manual on your desk along with a cover letter telling you to read and follow the manual. The normal reaction is to mutter a few unkind remarks about the manual's creator, throw the letter in the wastebasket, and stick the manual on the shelf to gather dust.

A much more effective technique is to introduce the manual to its users in a training session. Such sessions ensure that users look at the manual and acquire a general understanding of its contents. Aside from this practical value, the training sessions demonstrate to employees that the company is committed to the manual and expects it to be used.

Conducting Effective Training Sessions

To conduct an effective training session for users, follow these guidelines:

1. If possible, train users in groups of 20 or less. Employees are more likely to ask questions in a small group. Meetings with large groups quickly become formal presentations where employees grow bored and let their attention wander.

2. Keep the session informal and encourage group participation. People pay more attention when they're able to participate, so encourage everyone to ask questions. And if the group is too quiet, call on people and ask them questions.

3. Plan the sessions so each training group is composed of employees at approximately the same job level and with similar interests. Then you can structure the sessions to focus on each group's particular needs. For example, with a new office procedures manual, you might have separate sessions for supervisors and clerical employees. Each session would focus on the information most relevant to that particular group.

A further advantage to this approach is that employees do not attend the same sessions as their bosses. Consequently, both groups feel much more comfortable and are more likely to ask questions.

4. Hold the training session for managers before the sessions for employees. Otherwise, managers may be unprepared to answer employees' questions about the manual and may give out incorrect information. Also, it's common courtesy, as well as good sense, to inform managers first and then work downward in the organizational hierarchy.

5. Distribute the manuals at the training session, not ahead of time. If you distribute copies in advance, some people may skip the session.

6. Conduct the sessions in a setting free from interruptions. A company conference room or training facility is an appropriate choice. If you don't have such a room, you might reserve the company cafeteria for the meeting. Or you might use a meeting room in a hotel or other off-company site.

7. Plan the sessions carefully. Make arrangements ahead of time for any audiovisual aids and for coffee, tea, and soft drinks for the attendees.

8. Begin the meeting promptly, even if all attendees are not present. If you establish a reputation for late starts, people will

begin arriving even later. And it's only fair to those people who arrived on time to begin on time.

If you do not have a great deal of material to present, the meeting may take only one or two hours. However, if you are introducing a whole new system, the meeting may last all day, or you may schedule a series of sessions for each group. If the meeting will last over two hours, plan on a short break every hour or so. Most people aren't used to sitting for extended periods.

9. Inform the attendees well in advance of the meeting time and place. Some schedule conflicts may arise, so don't be surprised if you end up scheduling a "makeup" session. And use common sense in scheduling. For example, it would make no sense to schedule the managers' session the day before their quarterly budget reviews are due.

What to Cover in the Training Sessions

Now that you know how to plan and conduct the session, your next question probably is "What do I cover in the training session?" Obviously, the type of manual and the user's level of familiarity with the subject will do much to determine the content of your presentation. However, certain areas should be covered in any training session.

Introduce the group to the manual by discussing the material in the introductory section. Discuss the organization of the manual as shown in the table of contents. Explain how to use the index as a reference tool. And review the "how to use this manual" section so users will understand the format and be aware of any special aids in the manual, such as a glossary or forms section. It's also a good idea to discuss the user's responsibility to follow the manual, keep it up to date, and return it upon leaving the organization.

In your presentation, emphasize any changes in policies or procedures that are introduced in the manual. Often much of the manual is simply a formal statement of common knowledge. This material can be quickly reviewed. However, you should highlight any changes or new policies; do not expect users to discover them on their own.

If you're introducing a new system, demonstrate it. For example, if your company has just installed a new computer system, have a terminal at the session and show users how the system works. If the system involves forms, distribute samples to the participants and use an overhead or slide projector to demonstrate how the forms are completed. Use examples throughout your presentation to help users understand the material.

As a final part of the presentation, explain how and to whom users can submit corrections and suggestions for change. Stress the fact that you welcome feedback. You may want to conclude the session with an informal discussion. If you're not thoroughly familiar with the subjects covered in the manual, have some experts present to answer questions.

What to Do If You Can't Hold a Training Session

Sometimes it's impossible to introduce the manual in training sessions. If the manual's users are scattered across the country, you may have to mail the manuals to the users without a formal presentation. In this case, prepare a cover letter explaining what the manual is and a short "fact sheet" highlighting the topics you would normally cover in the training session. The fact sheet should explain:

How to use the table of contents and index.
The contents of the "how to use this manual" section.
Key aspects of the manual's contents.
How to suggest changes and corrections.

You may want to use a question-and-answer format for the fact sheet, as in this example:

> *Question:*   Whom do I notify of an error in the manual?
> *Answer:*   Ursula Update, procedures analyst.

If possible, include a "hot line" phone number that users can call if they have questions. And to build interest, publicize the manual in your employee newsletter or other corporate publication.

If there are any corporate gatherings such as conventions or regional meetings, take advantage of them to promote the manual. For example, one company whose agents were located all over the country set up a booth at its annual convention to promote the manual and several other projects. The company also promoted the manual during agent visits to corporate headquarters. Although these approaches aren't as effective as training sessions, they are viable alternatives when you cannot conduct training sessions—and they do increase use of the manuals.

MEASURING YOUR MANUAL'S EFFECTIVENESS

After the manual has been introduced to its users, your next task is to measure its effectiveness. There are two basic ways to determine if a manual is doing its job.

The first method, quantitative analysis, is applicable only if a manual introduces a new system or deals with operational procedures. Here you may be able to identify and measure some aspects of performance. For example, with a new inventory or accounting system, you might isolate these quantitative factors: time elapsed before the system runs smoothly, number of errors made in a specified time period, cost savings, and time required to train employees in the system.

Of course, you cannot apply quantitative standards to all manuals. It is extremely difficult to measure quantitatively the effectiveness of an employee handbook, personnel manual, or corporate policy manual. In this case your only option is to measure the manual's effectiveness qualitatively.

The best way to measure qualitative effectiveness is through a user survey, and the easiest way to conduct the survey is to administer a brief (one-page) questionnaire. Even if you can measure the manual's effectiveness quantitatively, you should measure it qualitatively as well to determine the level of user satisfaction.

To motivate your users to reply, keep the questionnaire as simple as possible and design it so it can be answered quickly and easily. Whenever possible, have boxes that can be checked and keep the amount of writing required to a minimum. Print your name and department on the reverse of the sheet so that the user can return the questionnaire by folding it in half, stapling it, and dropping it in the interdepartmental mail.

Figure 11 is a sample user questionnaire. Naturally the questions asked will depend on the type of manual you have prepared. However, the questions on the sample will give you a starting point to work from.

Conduct the mail survey about six weeks after the training sessions (or six weeks after distribution if there are no training sessions). This will give users enough time to become familiar with the manual, but not enough time to forget its existence.

Normally only 20 to 40 percent of the recipients return a mail survey. You may get a somewhat higher response if your survey is

Figure 11. Sample questionnaire.

Name _____ Dept. _____ Date _____

Please answer the following questions about the _____ manual. Your candid comments will help us evaluate the manual and improve its effectiveness.

Check the appropriate box and write any additional comments in the space provided.

1. Have you used the index to find any information?   □ Yes   □ No
   If so, was it easy to find what you wanted?
   □ Very easy   □ Fairly easy   □ Rather difficult   □ Very difficult

2. Do you understand the numbering system in the manual?
   □ Yes   □ No
   What does this number _____ represent? _____

3. Are the pages attractively designed and easy to read?.
   □ Very easy   □ Fairly easy   □ Fairly difficult   □ Very difficult

4. Is the writing clear and easy to understand?   □ Yes   □ No

5. How frequently do you use the manual?
   □ Every day   □ Three or more times a week
   □ Once or twice a week   □ One to three times a month   □ Never

6. How helpful is the manual in performing your job?
   □ Very helpful   □ Fairly helpful   □ Not very helpful

7. Have you found any errors in the manual?   □ Yes   □ No
   If so, what? _____
   _____

8. Do you have any suggestions for changes or improvements?
   _____
   _____
   _____

THANK YOU FOR COMPLETING THIS SURVEY!

Please fold the survey in half with your answers on the inside, staple it, and return it in the interdepartmental mail.

well-designed and is sent within the company. Whatever your response level, it is a good idea to conduct a random phone survey of some of the nonrespondents. Select a number of nonrespondents at random (at least 15 percent; more if you have time). Then call each person, explain that you have not received a survey response, and ask if you may conduct the survey over the phone. Although phone surveys are time-consuming, the advantages more than justify the additional effort. Phone surveys increase the statistical validity of the data and demonstrate your commitment to the manual. Users are impressed that you care enough to follow up on nonrespondents. If they haven't looked at the manual yet, they're likely to now because you've awakened their interest.

Conduct the phone survey approximately two weeks after the mail survey. By that time, you will have received virtually all the mail response that you're going to get.

After you complete the mail and phone surveys, prepare a brief report summarizing your findings. In the report, you may also find it helpful to correlate frequency of use with job position. A low frequency of use does not necessarily mean the manual is unsuccessful. Some users simply have a relatively low need to refer to the manual. It's also a good idea to send users a short summary of the survey findings and to inform them of any action you plan to take as a result of the survey. Then users know the time they spent completing the survey was not wasted.

In addition to being a valuable source of information, the survey motivates users by tangibly demonstrating the organization's commitment to the manual. When the survey arrives, users are once again reminded of the manual's importance.

It's a good idea to conduct the survey annually to measure any changes in user attitudes and perceptions. In the annual survey, the question on frequency of use is particularly valuable. It helps you accurately determine which employees need their own copies of the manual and which need only access to a departmental copy. The annual survey also enables you to determine new employees' reactions to the manual.

CHAPTER 13

Revisions and Updates: An Essential Part of the Manual's Development

A MANUAL is never finished. Even after you've distributed the copies and trained the users, much remains to be done. The odds are very good that even as the manual was being printed some of the information in it became obsolete. In most organizations, change occurs so rapidly that it is an ongoing battle to keep manuals up to date.

If a manual is not updated, the time and money spent developing it have been wasted. Within two years after its distribution, the manual will be virtually worthless. At least 30 percent of the information will be inaccurate—and no one will know which 30 percent. Consequently, the manual loses credibility. To prevent obsolescence, you should plan for updates and revisions when you begin preparing the manual. And as soon as the manual is released, you should begin your updating program.

Updates fall into two categories: irregular (unscheduled) and regular (scheduled). Let's consider irregular updates first, since most organizations do perform these occasionally.

HANDLING THE IRREGULAR UPDATE

Most organizations issue updates as the need arises. Perhaps the board of directors has established a new policy or revised an existing one to comply with new legislation. Or perhaps a procedure has been changed for safety reasons. Whatever the circumstances, your responsibility is to get the new material to users as quickly as possible.

Ideally, you will have already prepared a PERT chart outlining the necessary steps for issuing an update to the manual. Such a chart gives you a plan to follow and ensures that, if necessary, the process can begin in your absence. Usually the chart is a "mini" version of the PERT chart for the entire manual. It includes such steps as collecting necessary information, writing or rewriting the material, and getting it approved, printed, and distributed. Steps that do not apply (such as ordering binders and obtaining printing estimates) are omitted.

The major obstacle to the updating process is getting the revision approved. It's a good idea to establish a revision approval process in advance and to negotiate standard deadlines with reviewers so you don't have to set up a new schedule each time. The schedule might be three days' review time for revisions of three pages or less, a week for revisions of four to six pages, and a maximum of two weeks for longer updates. Be flexible in your scheduling. Explain to the reviewers that if circumstances prevent them from meeting a deadline, they should let you know so you can adjust your plans accordingly.

For urgent updates that must be released as quickly as possible, you have two options. The first is to release a temporary version of the policy or procedure. This version has not gone through the full review process and will remain in effect only until the final policy or procedure is issued. If you follow this approach, it's a good idea to print the temporary version on colored paper so users can easily identify it as an interim document. The final version will be printed on the same color paper as the rest of the manual (usually white).

Releasing a temporary version is a good approach when time is critical and the existing review structure is very complex. The major drawbacks to this approach are that (1) it doubles your printing costs and (2) it requires extra time on your part, since you must complete the revision twice.

Your second option for urgent revisions is to develop a streamlined version of the standard revision process. Some ways to save time include:

Hand-delivering the material to the reviewers, the printer, and other personnel as needed.

Having reviewers commit to a same-day review for urgent revisions.

Arranging for the urgent revision to be printed on a priority basis by the print shop.

Making the revision a top-priority item for you and your staff.

This streamlined approach has several advantages over the temporary notice system. The material is printed only once, and you spend less time on the revision. However, complete cooperation from everyone is essential. Also, you must be sure the system is used only on *urgent* revisions. Both the reviewers and the printer will resent having to rush for a revision that is not critical. After a few "false alarms," cooperation will disappear.

CONDUCTING THE REGULAR UPDATE

Although most organizations occasionally issue irregular updates, few update their manuals on a regular basis. You probably take your car in for a tuneup even though it appears to be running well, and you go to the doctor for an annual checkup even though you feel fine. You should be doing the same thing for your manuals by giving them a thorough regular review—even though you are unaware of any problems.

You should conduct a regular review of all manuals at least once a year. If the material changes rapidly, you may find it necessary to schedule the reviews twice a year. To conduct the review, send a copy of the material in the manual to the person qualified to determine if it is still accurate. With most manuals, different sections or topics will go to different people. Ask each person to review the material and indicate any changes or corrections.

It's a good idea to ask the reviewer to initial each page to ensure that the reviewer actually looks at the material. Otherwise, the reviewer may simply read your cover memo, say "I'm sure there are no changes," and sign off without even looking at the material.

You should also have your legal staff review the manual annually.

What was legal last year may not be legal this year, and you may be unaware of the change.

SCHEDULING THE REGULAR REVIEW

You may find it more convenient to schedule the regular review in sections rather than attempting to overhaul the entire manual at once. For example, if your manual has twelve sections and you are planning an annual review, review a section a month. This type of extended scheduling makes it easier to coordinate the review. It becomes a part of your work schedule instead of a major annual project that is easy to postpone or delay. Also, by doing the review in sections, you place less of a strain on the reviewers and the print shop.

Once the regular review becomes an ongoing program, you will find that your manuals remain effective. You no longer have to worry about whether users are keeping you posted on all changes. Finally, the regular review is one more way to motivate users. Once again you demonstrate that the manual is not a one-time project but an ongoing program. Users clearly understand their responsibility in keeping the manual up to date and recognize your commitment to the program.

TIPS FOR UPDATING

Whether the update is regular or irregular, you have a responsibility to communicate the new material effectively and to keep accurate records of all changes. Here are some ways to meet that responsibility.

When you are issuing revised material for the manual, indicate to users which portions have changed and which are still the same. The best way to indicate a change is to place a vertical line next to the material on the left-hand side. Then employees do not have to reread the entire policy on travel, for example, to find out that the company will now reimburse them 22 cents a mile for use of their personal cars on company business. The line looks like this:

1. When employees use their personal cars on company business, the company will reimburse the employee 22 cents for each mile traveled.

2. The company will also reimburse the employee for all parking expenses and tolls incurred while on company business.

With this system the user can easily see that the second and third lines of item 1 are the only material that has been changed.

Some organizations use an asterisk, arrow, or other symbol instead of a vertical line. However, a line is less obtrusive and indicates clearly the extent of the revisions. An asterisk or other symbol at the beginning of a paragraph does not tell you where the change occurred.

If you are issuing several revisions and updates at once, attach a summary sheet highlighting the main points of each update. Then if users don't have time to read through all the new material, they will at least be aware of the high points and know where to go for additional information. Print the summary sheet on brightly colored paper and use a bold heading to catch the reader's attention. Users do not need to keep the summary sheets or file them in their manuals.

Summary sheets and vertical lines aid the user in understanding the manual. Two other tips for updating will aid you, the preparer of the manual.

First, keep accurate records of all changes made to the manual (or changes that were rejected) and the reasons why. This file will be a valuable aid both to you and to those who follow in your footsteps. If good records aren't kept, you or your successor could easily repeat a past error or waste valuable time exploring a possibility that has already proved unfeasible.

Second, keep a copy of every manual page that was ever issued along with a record of when it was effective. These copies are important for legal reasons. With the increasing amount of litigation companies must face, it occasionally becomes necessary for the organization to be able to prove that a specific policy was or was not in effect at a particular time.

If your organization uses microfilm in its records management program, you should consider filming these earlier manual pages. Microfilm is convenient and saves space. In the absence of a printed copy, the film is legally acceptable as evidence in most instances. However, you should get your lawyer's approval before you keep only microfilm copies of any record.

MOTIVATING USERS TO KEEP THEIR MANUALS UP TO DATE

No matter how good a job you do of keeping the manual up to date, your efforts are meaningless unless users put the updates in their manuals and follow them. Motivating users to update their manuals is a problem that all preparers of manuals face. Countless approaches have been tried without success. I know of only two techniques that are really effective in motivating users. Both are "hard sell" approaches that require top management approval and support.

The first technique is incorporating a review of the manuals into your internal audit procedures. The auditors spot-check employees' manuals to determine if updates have been filed properly and record their findings in the audit report. This practice clearly demonstrates the value the organization places on its manuals and allows you to use a function that already exists in the organization. The internal audit is the most effective technique you can use, because auditors can usually be depended on to make a thorough and accurate report and because their reports have "clout."

The second method for ensuring user updating is to include a check of manuals as part of the performance appraisal process. This approach is designed for companies that do have an internal audit function or that cannot use it to check manuals. With this system, the supervisor makes a random sampling to see if updates issued since the last appraisal have been filed properly in the manual. The supervisor's findings are included in employee's performance appraisal.

As a corollary to this check, the employee's job description should include a statement that the employee is responsible for keeping up to date all manuals received and for obeying the policies and procedures stated in those manuals. This statement justifies including a check of the manuals in the performance appraisal. Employees know from the beginning that their manuals will be checked and that the results of the check will affect their performance review.

This technique is less satisfactory than the audit approach because there is no way to ensure that all supervisors check their employees' manuals. If a supervisor is lazy or overworked, he or she may not make the check. The system works best in small organizations where tight control can be maintained over the process.

If you are concerned about whether users actually receive the updates, send out a summary memo two to four times a year telling employees which updates and revisions they should have received and whom they should contact for copies if any updates are missing. If updates are being mailed to users, the summary memo is especially important. In addition to giving users the opportunity to check the accuracy of their manuals, the memo reminds users once again of the existence of the manuals and their importance to the company.

Some organizations have employees sign and return a form indicating that the updates were received. While this system does give the company proof that an employee received the update, it has some definite drawbacks. First, keeping track of the receipts can be practically a full-time job, especially if there are many users or if updates are frequent. Second, the return of a receipt is not proof that the update has been filed. Some employees may blithely sign and return the receipt and equally happily file the updates in their wastebaskets. To avoid this problem you can have users return the pages that were replaced. However, this approach further increases the amount of paperwork for your staff.

The best way to motivate users to update the manual *and* to use it is to prepare a manual that is attractive, well designed, easy to refer to, and easy to read—in short, a manual that answers its users' questions. If you have followed the guidelines in this book, you have all the tools you need to prepare and maintain just such a manual. The rest is up to you. Good luck!

Index

research, as data collection method, 17–18

responsibility, in playscript technique, 68

responsibility for manual production, 5–6

retrieval, of personal manuals, 106

review, in planning for policy manual, 7

review of manuals, as updating check, 122–123

review technique, working outline as, 27

reviewer
  initialing of pages by, 91
  legal staff as, 86
  responsibilities of, 87–88
  selection of, 85
  user as, 86

reviewer relations, as advantage of single editor, 8

reviewers, as personnel time costs, 15

review form, for review process, 91

review process
  changes as result of, 88
  deadlines in, 88–90
  legal review, as part of, 86
  personnel selection for, 85–87
  reviewer's responsibilities in, 87–88
  review form for, 91
  scheduling of, 92
  sectional approach to, 91
  time allowance in, 91

revision approval process, establishing, 118

Roget's International Thesaurus (Roget), as writing reference, 66

sample forms, use of, 80–82

scheduling of interviews, 19

scope of policy manual, statement of, 7–8

sectional approach, in review process, 91

section page numbering, 34

security, as reason for manual control, 105

sentence length, as affecting clarity, 64

serif vs. sans-serif type face, 37

setting, for interviews, 19–20

"(s)he," use of, as solution to he/she controversy, 65

shipping, of manuals, 100–101

shrink-wrapping binders, 45

signatures, use of, in standard headings, 38–39

special forms section, as visual support technique, 80

staff, role of, 8

standard page headings
  color printing of, 39
  company logo in, 39
  emphasizing items in, 39
  inclusions in, 38
  lines in, 39
  multi-page policies and, 40
  placement of information in, 39
  proper names in, 38
  signatures in, 38–39
  simplicity of, 39

standard paper stock, use of, 46

step-by-step listing, 67–68
  use of, in action-condition technique, 78

storage of manuals, 101–102

streamlined version, as manual updating, 118–119

subject, use of, in action-condition technique, 70

subject definition, as policy manual planning, 7

table of contents
  arrangement of, 50
  definition of, 49
  detail in, 50
  format references in, 50